The Ultimate
Disney Trivia
Book 4

Other books by Kevin Neary and Dave Smith

The Ultimate Disney Trivia Book
The Ultimate Disney Trivia Book 2
The Ultimate Disney Trivia Book 3

Other books by Dave Smith

Disney A to Z: The Official Encyclopedia
Disney: The First 100 Years
(with Steven Clark)

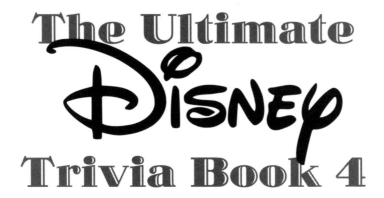

The Ultimate Disney Trivia Book 4

Kevin Neary
and Dave Smith

EDITIONS

New York

Library of Congress Cataloging-in-Publication Data

Neary, Kevin.
    The ultimate Disney trivia book 4 / Kevin Neary and
Dave Smith.
        p. cm.
    ISBN 0-7868-8529-7
    1. Walt Disney Company—Miscellanea.
I. Title: Ultimate Disney trivia book four.
II. Smith, Dave, 1940-
III. Walt Disney Company. IV. Title.
NC1766.U52 D554252000
384'.8'06579494—dc21   00-20369

FIRST EDITION

10 9 8 7 6 5 4 3 2 1

Contents

Introduction

by Dave Smith, Archives Director,
The Walt Disney Company

It has been three years since the appearance of *The Ultimate Disney Trivia Book 3*, and eight years since the first volume in 1992. We are now pushing into the new millennium, and The Walt Disney Company has never been more active.

Since the last trivia book, *The Lion King* has opened on Broadway, becoming one of the most popular musicals there in many a decade. *The Wonderful World of Disney* returned to television, and *One Saturday Morning* on ABC provided a home for a wide range of animated series. A new Tomorrowland debuted at Disneyland Park. Light Magic came and went at Disneyland, and the Main Street Electrical Parade returned to the Magic Kingdom at the Walt Disney World Resort. Also in Florida, Downtown Disney West Side helped provide nighttime entertainment, and Disney's Coronado Springs Resort added lodging with a Spanish Colonial atmosphere. Disney's Animal Kingdom became the fourth gated park at Walt Disney World, bringing guests close encounters with wildlife of Africa and Asia.

Disney entered the cruise business with the introduction of the *Disney Magic* and the *Disney Wonder*. The company made new inroads on the Internet with the launch of the GO Network. Popular movies included *Armageddon, The Horse Whisperer, Mulan, Mighty Joe Young, Inspector Gadget, The Sixth Sense,* and *Tarzan. Felicity* and *Once and Again* were among the successful series on television. On cable two new networks, Toon Disney and SoapNet, were launched. As the century drew to a close and the new one began, Epcot became the focal point for the company's Millennium Celebration, *Fantasia/2000* opened in IMAX Theaters, and construction proceeded on Disney's California Adventure and Tokyo DisneySea.

So, a lot has happened in just three years, and all this activity has enabled us to come up with 999 new questions about the world of Disney. As before, Kevin Neary originally wrote the vast majority of the questions, with me adding a few, doing some rewriting, and helping to ensure that the questions were accurate and unambiguous.

Kevin Neary has remained on the staff at Walt Disney World, doing work for Walt Disney Imagineering in addition to his duties with Disney Vacation Development. I am approaching my thirtieth anniversary as director of the Walt Disney Archives. Last fall I wrote, with coauthor Steven Clark, *Disney: The First 100 Years*, and in 1998 Hyperion published an updated edition of my *Disney A to Z: The Official Encyclopedia*. I continue a regular letters column in *Disney Magazine*. Kevin and I have both presented programs for passengers aboard the *Disney Magic*.

Kevin and I are delighted to have had the continued support of Disney fans everywhere for our series of trivia books. From Disney Store and theme park cast members and other Disney employees worldwide, from regular visitors to the parks, and from those who just like to watch the old Disney films on video, we have had frequent requests for a fourth trivia book. We hope that you will enjoy our latest effort and find these new trivia questions challenging.

In the tradition of our three previous books, this book again includes a total of 999 questions. Just like the Haunted Mansion, which claims to have 999 happy haunts and always room for one more, there is always room for one more trivia question.

Acknowledgments

The task of compiling a Disney trivia book cannot be accomplished without the advice and help from friends and colleagues. We would like to especially thank Steven Clark, Rebecca Cline, Tyson Ervin, Collette Espino, Shelly Graham, Wendy Lefkon, Adina Lerner, Michael Maney, James and Veronica Neary, Susan Neary, Veronica Owens, Darryl Pickett, Andrea Recendez, Mark Rhodes, Steven Rodriguez, Russell Schroeder, Clay Shoemaker, Paula Sigman-Lowery, Ed Squair, Andrew Swailes, Frank Thoma, Rich Thomas, Robert Tieman, and Laurel Whitcomb.

Animated Cartoons And Featurettes

....

Questions:

1. What American publisher first published the "Winnie the Pooh" stories?

2. Who is quoted as saying, "Mickey was simply a little personality assigned to the purposes of laughter"?

3. In the 1928 animated cartoon *The Gallopin' Gaucho* Mickey portrays a South American cowboy and spoofs what famous silent film star?

4. What musical instrument does Mickey play for a group of ghosts in the 1929 animated cartoon *The Haunted House*?

5. What is the first cartoon to depict Mickey Mouse and Minnie Mouse at the actual size of mice?

6. In the 1930 animated cartoon *The Picnic*, how does Pluto, who was then known as Rover, save the day after a sudden rainstorm erupts?

7. What 1930 Mickey short was originally copyrighted under the title *Fiddlin' Around*?

8. In which 1931 animated cartoon does Minnie demonstrate her love of gardening?

9. Name one of the two Mickey cartoons that are loosely based on the book *Robinson Crusoe* by author Daniel Defoe.

10. What song does Minnie Mouse play on the organ in the 1931 animated cartoon *Mickey's Orphans*?

11. What is the name of the Mickey animated short released to coincide with the 1932 Summer Olympic Games in Los Angeles?

12. Walter Lantz, originator of the Woody Woodpecker character, for many years produced cartoons featuring what early animated character created by Walt Disney?

13. For which classic 1933 animated short did it apparently take Walt Disney approximately six months to persuade his staff of animators that it was a workable project?

14. Of which classic animated short did Walt Disney remark, "At last we have achieved true personality in a whole picture"?

15. As what kind of animal does the Big Bad Wolf disguise himself in an effort to enter Fiddler Pig's home?

16. In *Three Little Pigs* (1933), after the Big Bad Wolf is unsuccessful at breaking down the front door of Practical Pig's home, how does he then decide to enter?

17. What is the name of the town the Pied Piper helps rid of rodents in the 1933 Silly Symphony by that same name?

18. What is unusual about the dog in the 1933 Silly Symphony *Lullaby Land*?

19. What is Mickey's profession in the classic animated cartoon *Building a Building* (1933)?

20. In the 1933 animated short *Puppy Love*, Mickey and Minnie perform a duet on what musical instrument?

21. What happens to the candy Mickey has for Minnie in the 1933 animated cartoon *Puppy Love*?

22. What is the name of the fictitious Hollywood motion picture Mickey and Minnie attend in the 1933 animated classic *Mickey's Gala Premiere*?

23. Walt Disney received his second Academy Award for Best Cartoon for which animated short?

24. Which 1933 Silly Symphony features a wooden toy of Mickey Mouse riding a scooter?

25. What was the 1934 animated character whose voice preceded his creation?

26. What was the first book published that featured Donald Duck?

27. In the classic 1934 animated cartoon *Grasshopper and the Ants*, who warns the grasshopper that he will certainly change his thinking when winter arrives?

28. What did the most famous children's lunch box featuring Disney characters resemble?

29. Name one of the Disney animated cartoon sequels in which the Big Bad Wolf captures two of the pigs.

30. In the 1936 animated cartoon *Alpine Climbers*, with what breed of dog does Pluto partake of some brandy?

31. What kind of animal chases Hiawatha at the conclusion of the 1937 animated cartoon *Little Hiawatha*?

32. In the animated cartoon *Ferdinand the Bull* (1938), what turns the peaceful bull into a raging beast?

33. In the 1939 animated classic *Donald's Cousin Gus,* what does Donald feed his cousin Gus Goose causing his stomach to bark?

34. Who is quoted as saying, "It is the constitutional privilege of every American to become cultured or grow up like Donald Duck"?

35. True or false: opinions about Mickey Mouse among Axis leaders during World War II were mixed.

36. In 1942, Donald officially enlisted in *Donald Gets Drafted.* How long did it take for the U.S. Army to officially discharge Private Donald?

37. Children's gas masks in England during World War II were made in the shape of what character?

38. Which two animated characters were named after an 18th-century furniture maker?

39. What is the title of the 1946 Academy Award-nominated short for Best Cartoon, which stars Mickey Mouse and Pluto with Chip and Dale?

40. In the 1951 animated cartoon *Lucky Number*, what does Donald actually win while thinking it is all a trick by his three nephews?

41. What 1952 cartoon depicts Goofy as Mr. Geef shown moving to an island paradise only to be thrown into a volcano to appease the fire goddess Pele?

42. In the 1952 animated short *Donald Applecore*, what are the first three lines of the rhyme game that Donald and Chip and Dale say to each other?

43. What does Dale disguise himself as in an attempt to avoid the curious Pluto while on the mantel in the Academy Award-nominated cartoon *Pluto's Christmas Tree* (1952)?

44. What actor provided the original voice for Piglet in the Winnie the Pooh animated featurettes?

45. Which characters are known as Tic and Tac in French?

46. What Disney character joined Tom Selleck to present the Academy Award for Best Animated Short at the 60th Academy Award Presentation in 1988?

47. Three Disney animated characters from what feature film presented the Academy Award for Best Animated Short at the 64th Academy Award Presentation in 1992?

48. What animated character experienced the longest gap in the number of years (forty-seven) between Academy Award nominations for Best Cartoon?

49. If Mickey is a mouse and Pluto a dog, what is Goofy?

50. Which animated character has appeared in more animated shorts over the years, Mickey Mouse or Donald Duck?

Animated Cartoons
and Featurettes

Answers:

1. In 1926 A. A. Milne's book *Winnie-the-Pooh* was published by E. P. Dutton & Company. Two years later, they released *The House at Pooh Corner*. In the seven decades that have passed, the two books have sold more than 14 million copies in twelve different languages.
2. Walt Disney.
3. Mickey spoofs silent film star Douglas Fairbanks.
4. Mickey is persuaded to play the organ for a group of ghosts.
5. *When the Cat's Away* (1929) represented the first and only occasion when Mickey and Minnie were depicted at the actual size of mice.
6. He uses his tail as a windshield wiper.
7. The animated short *Just Mickey* was originally copyrighted as *Fiddlin' Around*.
8. *Mickey Cuts Up.*
9. *The Castaway* (1931) and *Mickey's Man Friday* (1935) were both inspired by Defoe's story of *Robinson Crusoe*.
10. Minnie plays the Christmas carol "Silent Night" on the organ in *Mickey's Orphans*.
11. *Barnyard Olympics.*
12. When Walt Disney lost the rights to Oswald the Lucky Rabbit, the task of producing cartoons featuring the character eventually went to Walter Lantz.
13. It supposedly took Walt Disney approximately six months to persuade his artists that his idea for an animated story based on *Three Little Pigs* was a good one.
14. *Three Little Pigs* (1933).
15. The Big Bad Wolf disguises himself as a sheep.
16. The Big Bad Wolf decides to enter the house by going down the chimney but Practical Pig has a surprise for his unwanted guest in the form of a kettle on a blazing fire.
17. The town of Hamelin.
18. The little dog is a toy who romps around with his infant owner.
19. Mickey operates a steam shovel at a construction site.
20. The two perform a duet on the piano.

21. The dogs, Pluto and Fi Fi, eat the candy and Pluto places a bone in the candy box instead.

22. The name of the fictitious film is *Galloping Revue*.

23. Walt Disney received his second Academy Award for Best Cartoon for *Three Little Pigs* (1933).

24. In the 1933 Silly Symphony *The Night Before Christmas*, a wooden toy of Mickey Mouse riding a scooter is part of Santa's bag of toys.

25. Walt Disney heard a radio show in Los Angeles that featured Clarence Nash portraying several animals. Based on Nash's voice the character Donald Duck was created. Nash eventually went on to provide the voice of Donald Duck for the next fifty years.

26. In 1934, the book *The Wise Little Hen* was released. The book retold the story of the cartoon *The Wise Little Hen*, which was released on June 9, 1934, marking the debut of Donald. However, the *name* Donald Duck appeared in the text of *The Adventures of Mickey Mouse* (1931).

27. While the ants worked at preparing themselves for the upcoming cold and snowy winter, the grasshopper danced and played his fiddle. It was the Queen of the ant colony who assured the grasshopper that he would change his thinking when severe weather arrived.

28. The most popular lunch box ever produced was one by Aladdin Industries that resembled a school bus, featuring Goofy as the driver and some of the other characters as passengers. That particular lunch box was produced between 1961 and 1973 and over 9 million were sold.

29. *Three Little Wolves* (1936) or *The Practical Pig* (1939).

30. St. Bernard.

31. A bear.

32. A simple bee sting turns Ferdinand into a raging bull.

33. Donald feeds Gus what were called "Barking Hot Dogs." As one reads on the food package: "A sure way to get rid of hungry relatives."

34. Walt Disney.

35. True. Germany's Hitler hated him while Italy's Mussolini and Japan's Emperor Hirohito loved him.

36. In 1984, during the celebrations for Donald's fiftieth birthday, the U.S. Army created discharge papers for the feisty duck.

37. Mickey Mouse gas masks were made to help persuade children to carry them.

38. Chip and Dale were named after 18th-century furniture maker Thomas Chippendale.

39. *Squatter's Rights.*

40. Donald actually wins a car but when the nephews pick up the prize so they can surprise their uncle, he thinks it is a trick and proceeds to wreck the automobile.

41. *Hello, Aloha.*

42. The rhyme game that Donald and Chip and Dale say to each other in *Donald Applecore* is "Applecore ... Baltimore ... Who's your friend?" followed by one of them then getting smashed in the face with an apple. Donald always seems to be the one who gets smashed.

43. Dale disguises himself as a Santa candle.

44. Actor John Fiedler was the original voice of Piglet. Fiedler has also provided voices in such Disney films as *Robin Hood* (1973), *The Rescuers* (1977), and *The Fox and the Hound* (1981). Fiedler may best be remembered for playing the role of one of Dr. Robert Hartley's familiar patients, Mr. Emil Peterson, on the long-running comedy series *The Bob Newhart Show* (1972–1978).

45. Chip and Dale.

46. On April 11, 1988, Mickey Mouse and Tom Selleck presented the award for Best Animated Short.

47. On March 30, 1992, Chip, Belle, and the Beast from the animated feature *Beauty and the Beast* (1991) presented the award for Best Animated Short.

48. Mickey Mouse's cartoons went forty-seven years between Academy Award nominations. Mickey received an Academy Award nomination for Best Cartoon for the 1948 animated short *Mickey and the Seal*. It wasn't until 1995 and the animated short *Runaway Brain* that he received another nomination.

49. Just as Mickey is a humanized mouse (he walks on two legs and talks), Goofy is a humanized dog. His original name was Dippy Dawg. Pluto, however, is a dog whose four paws are firmly planted in the animal kingdom.

50. Donald has appeared in over 180 animated cartoons and Mickey has appeared in over 120. Remarkably, over 60 percent of the Mickey cartoons were produced by 1935 and were in black-and-white.

Comic
Characters

....

Questions:

1. In the 1939 comic strip *The Miracle Master,* what does Mickey discover in a curio shop?

2. In what year did Carl Barks begin drawing Donald Duck for comic books?

3. What was the first Donald Duck comic book story that Carl Barks drew, in cooperation with Jack Hannah?

4. In the classic Donald Duck comic story *Lost in the Andes*, what shape are the eggs that Donald and his nephews are trying to find?

5. What is the name of the gang of canine cons who first appeared in comic stories in 1951 and then later in the animated television series *Disney's Duck Tales*?

6. Which animated character was featured in his own comic series from 1953 to 1962 and then again in 1990 to 1997?

7. What is the name of the comic book series first published in 1954 and which featured Daisy Duck?

8. In a classic Disney comic strip, Donald Duck's three nephews helped him raise a sunken ship by what ingenious method?

9. What female relative of Donald Duck had her own comic book series?

Comic Characters

Answers:

1. Mickey discovers a magic lamp. Interestingly, this story has Minnie demonstrating a fascination for antiques, a hobby shared by Walt's wife, Lillian.
2. Carl Barks began drawing Donald Duck in comics in 1942.
3. *Donald Duck Finds Pirate Gold.* It was featured in Dell Four Color Comics, no. 9.
4. The eggs are square.
5. The canine con gang is known as the Beagle Boys.
6. Goofy.
7. The comic book series was known as *Daisy Duck's Diary.* The comic series dealt with shopping, primping, and keeping Donald in line. With the introduction of the comic book in 1954, Daisy became one of the few female characters to star in her own series.
8. The three filled the ship with Ping-Pong balls so the ship would float. The story inspired the method for an actual ship-raising many years later.
9. Grandma Duck.

Animated Features

....

Snow White and the Seven Dwarfs

December 21, 1937

Questions:

1. As the Dwarfs make their daily march back from the diamond mine to their cottage in what order are they?

2. What does the pessimistic Grumpy call the chicken dumplings that Snow White has prepared for them that first day at the Dwarfs' cottage?

3. When asked by Snow White if he had washed his hands for dinner, what does Sleepy reply?

4. Which of the Dwarfs was the last to make friends with Snow White?

5. What musical instrument does Grumpy play?

6. What is the Magic Mirror referring to when it says, "Over the seven jeweled hills, beyond the seventh fall"?

7. How many warts does the Queen, when disguised as the old peddler woman, have on her nose?

8. How many bites of the apple does Snow White take before falling victim to the Queen's spell?

9. Which of the Dwarfs was the shortest and which one was tallest?

10. In one animated segment that was originally planned for the film but not included in the final cut, what do the Dwarfs build for their guest, Snow White?

Snow White and the Seven Dwarfs

Answers:

1. Doc leads the march and he is followed by Grumpy, Happy, Sleepy, Bashful, Sneezy, and Dopey.
2. Always the pessimist, Grumpy refers to the stew as "witch's brew."
3. "It ain't summer!"
4. Grumpy was the last to make friends with Snow White and yet was the first to suggest she might be in danger from the Queen later in the film.
5. Grumpy plays the organ.
6. The Magic Mirror is referring to the location of the Dwarfs' cottage and the whereabouts of the Princess Snow White.
7. The Queen, when disguised as the old peddler woman, has one wart on her nose.
8. Snow White takes just one bite of the apple.
9. According to the model sheets developed to help animators create the look of each Dwarf, Dopey is slightly shorter and Doc is a little taller than the others. The remaining five Dwarfs are all the same size.
10. The Dwarfs construct an elaborate bed for Snow White, but during production Walt Disney decided to omit the sequence.

Pinocchio

February 7, 1940

Questions:

1. When translated into English, what does the name "Pinocchio" mean?

2. Which character initially dislikes the name Pinocchio when she first hears of it from Geppetto?

3. Which character says, "A very lovely thought but not at all practical"?

4. What song does Honest John sing to Pinocchio?

5. Finish the line, "A boy who won't be good might just as well be _____."

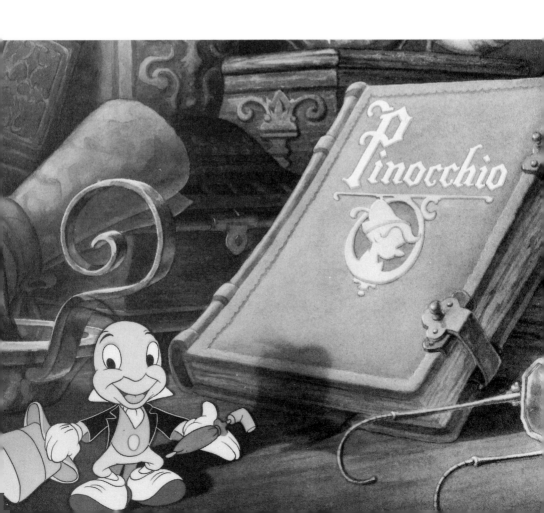

Pinocchio

Answers:

1. When translated into English from Italian, the name "Pinocchio" means loosely "little piece of pine" or "something little that comes from pine."
2. The fish, Cleo.
3. Jiminy Cricket makes the statement on hearing Geppetto make a wish, on the wishing star, for Pinocchio to become a real boy.
4. In an effort to keep Pinocchio from going to school, Honest John entices him with the song "Hi Diddle Dee Dee."
5. "A boy who won't be good might just as well be *made of wood.*" The line is spoken by the Blue Fairy.

Cinderella

February 15, 1950

Questions:

1. What song does Cinderella sing as she gets dressed in the morning?

2. What song do the mice and birds sing and whistle as they fashion an elegant gown for Cinderella so that she may attend the Royal Ball?

3. In one scene we see the King asleep. What is he dreaming about?

4. From which foot, right or left, does Cinderella lose her glass slipper?

5. What is the name of the Academy Award–nominated song from the film?

Cinderella

Answers:

1. "A Dream Is a Wish Your Heart Makes."
2. "The Work Song."
3. The King is dreaming about his future grandchildren.
4. In her haste to leave the palace, Cinderella loses the glass slipper from her left foot.
5. The Academy Award–nominated song from *Cinderella* (1950) is "Bibbidi-Bobbidi-Boo," with music and lyrics by Mack David, Al Hoffman, and Jerry Livingston.

Peter Pan

February 5, 1953

Questions:

1. Who does the jealous Tinker Bell tell to shoot Wendy down from the sky?

2. What word is on the tattoo that Mr. Smee has on his chest?

3. What group becomes jealous of Peter Pan's newfound friendship with Wendy and even attempts to drown her?

4. Who does Peter Pan tell the Lost Boys will be their mother?

5. What does Captain Hook offer the Darling children and the Lost Boys after they are captured by the captain's band of pirates?

Peter Pan

1. Tinker Bell tells the Lost Boys to shoot Wendy down because of her and Peter's newfound friendship. They call her a "Wendy Bird."
2. Mr. Smee's tattoo says "Mother."
3. The mermaids.
4. Wendy.
5. Captain Hook offers them their freedom and a free tattoo if they will join his crew of pirates.

Lady and the Tramp

June 22, 1955

Questions:

1. What character says, "A human heart has only so much room for love and affection. When a baby moves in, the dog moves out"?

2. Why were the dogs in the pound giving a playful rendition of the song "Home, Sweet Home" when Lady arrived?

3. What food do Lady and Tramp share when they go to Tony's Restaurant?

4. What two sets of initials appear in the cement heart when Lady and the Tramp spend that first evening together?

5. Which animated character in the feature *Lady and the Tramp* (1955) originally was referred to as Mame in the script?

Lady and the Tramp

Answers:

1. Tramp makes this statement to Lady on their first encounter.
2. They were attempting to cover up Dachsie's tunneling activity so no one would hear him dig.
3. The two share a plate of spaghetti and meatballs.
4. The initials are "J. M." and "E. B." No one knows why the Disney artists used these particular initials.
5. The dog, Peg, was originally referred to in the script as Mame. The name was changed so as not to offend first lady Mamie Eisenhower.

101 Dalmatians

January 25, 1961

Questions:

1. Which character opens the film by talking about his pet?

2. In the film, what color were Cruella De Vil's gloves?

3. Which of the Dalmatian puppies features spots in the shape of a horseshoe on his back?

4. Who is the last dog to relay the Twilight Bark on to the Colonel that fifteen puppies were stolen in London?

5. Why is Cruella De Vil's hair white on one side and black on the other?

101 Dalmatians

Answers:

1. The Dalmatian Pongo refers to his owner, Roger, as his pet.
2. Cruella wore red gloves.
3. Lucky features a series of spots shaped like horseshoes.
4. The hound dog Towser.
5. For the answer, one would have to consult Dodie Smith's original book, *The Hundred and One Dalmatians*. Cruella apparently drank ink as a child, which is the root of her hair problems.

The Aristocats

December 24, 1970

Questions:

1. What song does Berlioz play on the piano while he and Marie have their music lesson?

2. What does Edgar call the substance he puts into the cat food of Duchess and her three kittens so the four will fall unconscious, making the disposal of them easier?

3. After Thomas O'Malley rescues Duchess and her three kittens in the countryside, what type of vehicle do they board in order to get back to the city?

4. What actress provided the singing voice for the character Frou-Frou?

5. Which character picks the lock on the sealed trunk enabling Duchess and her kittens to escape from being shipped to Timbuktoo?

The Aristocats

Answers:

1. The two perform the song "Scales and Arpeggios."
2. Edgar refers to it as "crème de la crème à la Edgar."
3. The five hop on board the back of a milk truck.
4. Actress Ruth Buzzi provided the singing voice of the character Frou-Frou. Actress Nancy Kulp provides the speaking voice of the character. Kulp may best be remembered for playing the part of Miss Jane Hathaway on *The Beverly Hillbillies* (1962–1971).
5. Roquefort the mouse.

The Many Adventures of Winnie the Pooh

March 11, 1977

Questions:

1. According to Pooh, what condition will improve if he exercises?

2. Instead of a traditional cuckoo clock, what pops out from Winnie the Pooh's clock?

3. Besides honey, what other two food items does Winnie the Pooh sing about in his song?

4. How does Rabbit spell the word "carrots" on a sign in his garden?

5. What do the letters "T.T.F.N." stand for when Tigger says good-bye?

6. Where does Winnie the Pooh go to do all of his thinking?

7. Who is Roo's best friend?

8. What song does everyone sing during the hero party Christopher Robin organizes?

9. What does Christopher Robin say he prefers doing best?

10. What kind of animal is Piglet?

The Many Adventures of Winnie the Pooh

Answers:

1. Pooh says that his appetite would improve by exercising.
2. Instead of a cuckoo clock, Pooh has a "Pooh-coo Clock" and a little Pooh pops out in a tiny honey jar.
3. Besides honey, Pooh sings about milk and chocolate.
4. Rabbit spells the word "carrots" as "kerits."
5. "T.T.F.N." stands for "Ta Ta For Now."
6. Pooh goes to his Thoughtful Spot to do all of his thinking.
7. Roo's best friend is Tigger.
8. The characters sing "Hip Hip Pooh-Ray."
9. "Nothing at all."
10. This is an easy one: Piglet is a small pig.

The Little Mermaid

November 17, 1989

Questions:

1. Once Ariel agrees to give up her voice so that she can become human, where does the evil Ursula place it for safekeeping?

2. According to the song "Under the Sea," where will fish find themselves when the boss gets hungry?

3. What means of transportation do Ariel and Prince Eric take during their tour of the kingdom?

4. Who provides the voice of Prince Eric?

5. What kind of creature is the evil sea witch Ursula?

The Little Mermaid

Answers:

1. Ursula places Ariel's voice inside a shell, which hangs around her neck.
2. "On the plate."
3. The two ride in a horse-drawn carriage to tour Prince Eric's kingdom.
4. The voice of Eric was provided by Christopher Daniel Barnes, who was at that time the U.S. National Teenage Spokesperson for the environmental organization known as Greenpeace.
5. Ursula is an octopus.

Beauty and the Beast

November 13, 1991

Questions:

1. Who is the most important person Gaston neglects to inform about his planned wedding?

2. How many eggs does Gaston eat every day?

3. What convinces Belle, on her first day in the castle, that the place is enchanted?

4. Which song includes the line, "Try the gray stuff, it's delicious. Don't believe me, ask the dishes?"

5. What becomes of the gargoyles that adorn the Beast's castle after his transformation back into the Prince?

Beauty and the Beast

Answers:

1. Gaston addresses the townspeople: "I'd like to thank you all for coming..." The only problem is that he hasn't asked Belle for her hand in marriage yet.

2. According to Gaston's song, "When I was a lad I ate four dozen eggs every morning to help me get large. Now that I'm grown I eat five dozen eggs so I'm roughly the size of a barge." One can only venture to guess his cholesterol level!

3. Meeting a talking candlestick and mantel clock gives Belle a pretty good indication that she is in an enchanted castle.

4. "Be Our Guest."

5. The gargoyles turn back to their original shape, that of angels.

The Lion King

June 24, 1994

Questions:

1. Who does Simba refer to as "banana beak"?

2. Which song does Simba sing about what life will be like when he becomes king?

3. What are Pumbaa and Simba describing when they say "slimy yet satisfying"?

4. What popular song by the 1960s group The Tokens does Timon sing?

5. What character dresses up in a hula skirt in order to create a diversion?

The Lion King

Answers:

1. Simba refers to Zazu by the name "banana beak." However, Zazu is quick to point out that the name should be "Mr. Banana Beak."
2. "I Just Can't Wait to Be King."
3. He is describing part of that day's selection of bugs that he and Timon eat.
4. Appropriately, Timon sings The Tokens' classic "The Lion Sleeps Tonight."
5. Timon dons a hula skirt in order to fool and distract the hyenas.

Pocahontas

June 23, 1995

Questions:

1. In the animated feature *Pocahontas*, the song "Mine, Mine, Mine" has different meanings for the two characters, Governor Ratcliffe and Captain John Smith. What does the song mean for each of the two men?

2. What is the name of Governor Ratcliffe's smug little dog?

3. What is the name of Pocahontas's best friend in the tribe?

4. What becomes of the nasty Governor Ratcliffe at the conclusion of the film?

5. Do Pocahontas and Captain John Smith get the opportunity to continue their budding romance as the film concludes?

Pocahontas

Answers:

1. When Governor Ratcliffe sings the song "Mine, Mine, Mine," he is referring to all of the gold he believes awaits him. For Smith, the song refers to the adventure and discovery of a new and as yet uncharted land.
2. Percy is the name of Governor Ratcliffe's dog, a pug.
3. Nakoma is Pocahontas's best friend.
4. The nasty Governor Ratcliffe is imprisoned and taken back to England for his wrongdoing and his abuse of power.
5. Unfortunately, they don't get the opportunity because Captain John Smith is wounded and sent back to England to recover.

The Hunchback of Notre Dame

June 21, 1996

Questions:

1. What day of the year is celebrated as Topsy-Turvy Day?

2. With whom does Quasimodo fall in love?

3. Where is Esmeralda when she sings about the plight of her people in the song "God Help the Outcasts"?

4. What two characters travel to the Court of Miracles to warn the gypsies that Judge Frollo is planning to attack their secret location?

5. How do the two characters mentioned in question 4 above determine the secret whereabouts of the Court of Miracles?

The Hunchback
of Notre Dame

Answers:

1. January 6.
2. Quasimodo falls in love with the gypsy Esmeralda.
3. Esmeralda is inside the Cathedral of Notre Dame seeking sanctuary.
4. Phoebus and Quasimodo go to the Court of Miracles to warn the gypsies of Judge Frollo's plan, but the two are taken captive instead.
5. The location of the Court of Miracles is on a gypsy talisman that Esmeralda gave to Quasimodo. The talisman is a cleverly disguised map of the city of Paris.

Hercules

June 27, 1997

Questions:

1. Which Academy Award–winning actor provided the narration for the film's opening?

2. How many Muses are there?

3. The infant Hercules is given what type of animal as a pet?

4. What is Hercules' baby cradle made of while he is on Mount Olympus?

5. Why does Hades, ruler of the Underworld, want to destroy Hercules?

6. What type of mythological creature is Phil?

7. Megara and Hercules first meet after he saves her from the clutches of what evil creature?

8. What name does Phil use to describe the city of Thebes?

9. What multiheaded creature does Hercules battle with first to gain the respect of the citizens of Thebes and prove that he is truly a "hero"?

10. In an effort to save Meg from the evil clutches of Hades, what deal must Hercules strike with the ruler of the Underworld?

Hercules

Answers:

1. Charlton Heston.
2. Five; Calliope, Melpomene, Terpsichore, Thalia, and Clio.
3. A flying horse, Pegasus.
4. Hercules' baby cradle is made from a cloud.
5. Hades learns from the Fates that Hercules is the only person who stands between him and his takeover of Mount Olympus. (The Fates are three crones who have the ability to see into the future, present, and past and cut every mortal's thread of life, sending that person to the Underworld.)
6. Phil is a satyr—half man, half goat.
7. The Centaur Nessus.
8. Phil calls Thebes "the Big Olive," a reference to New York City's famous nickname, "the Big Apple."
9. The mythical creature is known as a Hydra. Unfortunately for Hercules, each time he uses his sword to cut a head off the Hydra, it grows back three more. Because of the complexity of the Hydra, it took fifteen Disney animators and technicians two years to create the five-minute film sequence.
10. In the deal, Hercules had to give up his legendary strength for a day.

Mulan

June 19, 1998

Questions:

1. Who is the leader of the Huns and what country has he invaded?

2. How do the people of China know they have been invaded by the Huns?

3. What is the name of Mulan's little dog and what chore does he do for her?

4. Why are they primping Mulan at the beginning of the film?

5. What is the name of the wisecracking dragon that accompanies Mulan?

6. What is the name of the supposedly lucky little cricket that joins Mulan on her journeys?

7. Which actor provided the voice of the Fa family's First Ancestor?

8. What name does Mulan assume after disguising herself as a man in order to take her father's place to fight the Huns?

9. How does Mulan single-handedly destroy almost the entire Hun army?

10. Which individuals provide the speaking voices and singing voices for the animated characters Mulan and Captain Li Shang?

Mulan

Answers:

1. The evil Shan-Yu is the leader of the Huns and he has invaded China.
2. Shan-Yu and his army cross over the Great Wall of China. Along the Great Wall signal torches are lit, indicating an invasion has taken place.
3. The dog's name is Little Brother and Mulan gets him to feed the chickens for her.
4. Mulan has an appointment to see the town's matchmaker in hopes of finding a husband. Unfortunately, nothing goes as planned for Mulan.
5. The dragon is Mushu, voiced by actor/comedian Eddie Murphy.
6. The little cricket is known as Cri-Kee.
7. The voice of the First Ancestor is that of George Takei. Takei may best be remembered for the character Lieutenant Sulu, which he played in the *Star Trek* television series and films.
8. Mulan takes the name "Ping."
9. Mulan takes the last cannon and fires it at a snow-covered mountain. The explosion from the cannon consequently causes a giant avalanche, which buries most of the Hun army.
10. The character Mulan's speaking voice was provided by actress Ming-Na Wen and her singing voice is that of Lea Salonga. Wen appeared in the 1993 Hollywood Pictures film *The Joy Luck Club*, and Salonga was the singing voice of Princess Jasmine in the 1992 animated feature *Aladdin*. Li Shang's speaking voice was provided by B. D. Wong and his singing voice is that of Donny Osmond. Wong may best be remembered for his role on Broadway in *M. Butterfly*; for Disney he played the part of Franck's assistant, Harry, in the *Father of the Bride* film series.

Tarzan

June 19, 1999

Questions:

1. What is the name of the nasty leopard that killed Tarzan's human parents?

2. Who serves as Tarzan's adoptive gorilla mother?

3. What is the name of the silverback gorilla who serves as the leader of the gorilla family?

4. What is the name of Tarzan's best gorilla friend and what popular actress provides the voice?

5. What is the name of the neurotic African elephant?

6. Where are Jane and her father, Professor Porter, from?

7. What is the name of the hunter and adventurer that Professor Porter and his daughter, Jane, hire to be their jungle guide?

8. What song do Terk and her friends perform while they destroy Jane and the professor's camp?

9. Professor Porter is a noted scientist who for years has been studying a certain type of animal even though he has never seen one in the wild. Name the animal that Professor Porter is seeking.

10. What becomes of Jane as the film concludes?

Tarzan

1. The leopard is named Sabor.
2. Tarzan's adoptive mother is Kala, voiced by actress Glenn Close.
3. The leader of the gorilla family is Kerchak.
4. Tarzan's best gorilla friend is Terk, voiced by actress and talk-show host Rosie O'Donnell. As a youngster, Terk is essentially Tarzan's protector. She is absolutely convinced he can't live without her.
5. Tantor.
6. Jane and her father are from London. Actress Minnie Driver provided the voice of the curious Jane, and actor Nigel Hawthorne provided the voice of Professor Porter. Hawthorne also provided the voice of Fflewddur Fflam in the 1985 Disney animated feature *The Black Cauldron.*
7. Professor Porter and his daughter Jane hire Clayton as their jungle guide. Unfortunately, the two mistake Clayton for a trusted confidant and don't discover Clayton's dark side until it is too late.
8. "Trashin' the Camp."
9. Professor Porter has studied gorillas all of his life, yet he has never seen one in the wild.
10. Jane and her father decide not to go back to London, but rather to stay in Africa with Tarzan and the rest of the gorilla family.

Fantasia/2000

January 1, 2000

Questions:

1. Where did *Fantasia/2000* hold its world premiere?

2. Which musical piece accompanies the *Noah's Ark* animated segment of the film?

3. Which Disney character is left with the task of ensuring that all the animals are aboard Noah's Ark in the animated segment by that same name?

4. The animated segment *The Steadfast Tin Soldier* is based on a story by what author?

5. What is the only animated segment that remains in *Fantasia/2000* from the 1940 version?

Fantasia/2000

Answers:

1. *Fantasia/2000* had its world premiere at Carnegie Hall in New York
    City on December 17, 1999. The premiere was accompanied by the
    Philharmonia Orchestra of London under the baton of conductor
    James Levine, with the 120-piece orchestra playing in synch with
    the film. The ensemble also embarked on a weeklong tour with
    performances at London's Royal Albert Hall, Paris' Theatre des
    Champs-Elysees, and Tokyo's Orchard Hall, then to California for
    a special New Year's Eve engagement. A *Fantasia/2000* gala took place
    at the Pasadena Civic Auditorium, where 2,000 invited guests greeted
    the turn of the century and the millennium with a live performance
    and screening of the film. Following the concert tour, the film began
    an exclusive four-month engagement at IMAX theaters around the
    world on January 1, 2000.
2. The musical piece that accompanies the *Noah's Ark* segment is
    "Pomp and Circumstance," by Sir Edward Elgar.
3. Donald is given the task of ensuring all of the animals are safely
    aboard Noah's Ark. At first, Donald cannot find Daisy; but after a
    frantic search, he is reunited with his sweetheart.
4. Hans Christian Andersen.
5. *The Sorcerer's Apprentice.*

Animated Feature Potpourri

....

Questions:

1. What story by author Washington Irving did Walt Disney consider as a possible film for his first full-length animated feature?

2. What early Disney film did the *New York Herald Tribune* call "one of those rare works of inspired artistry that weaves an irresistible spell around the beholder"?

3. What villainess did Walt Disney describe to his artists as "sinister, mature, with plenty of curves"?

4. What 1934 Silly Symphony was instrumental in the development of the Snow White character?

5. What did the women in Disney's Ink and Paint Department apply to each cel in order to give Snow White's cheeks an even rosier complexion?

6. True or false: The Queen from *Snow White and the Seven Dwarfs* (1937) was originally drawn as a stout, comedic type of character.

7. Prior to the release of *Snow White and the Seven Dwarfs* (1937), what animation studio produced its own version of the Snow White story?

8. The animated segment the *Pastoral Symphony* featured in *Fantasia* (1940) was originally intended to be combined with which musical piece by Gabriel Pierné?

9. What animated segment from *Fantasia* (1940) was at one point distributed to schools in an effort to teach children geology and paleontology?

10. What full-length animated feature was originally scheduled to be the studio's second release?

11. What 1943 full-length animated feature received the Academy Award nomination for Best Score?

12. In what full-length animated feature does Donald Duck learn about the Mexican children's procession at Christmastime known as *Las Posadas*?

13. What type of weapon is used by Peter in an attempt to capture the wolf in the animated segment *Peter and the Wolf* in the film *Make Mine Music* (1946)?

14. Why did Willie the Giant steal the Golden Harp in the animated segment *Mickey and the Beanstalk* from the 1947 full-length animated feature *Fun and Fancy Free*?

15. Willie the Giant from the 1947 full-length feature *Fun and Fancy Free* has a difficult time pronouncing what word in the film?

16. What full-length animated feature was inspired by a story that appeared in the book entitled *Tales from Mother Goose*?

17. "I'm in the Middle of a Muddle" was a song written for an animated feature but was never used. Which full-length animated feature was scheduled to include this song?

18. Which full-length animated feature includes the most songs?

19. What character from the feature *Alice in Wonderland* (1951) makes this statement?: "I give myself very good advice but I very seldom follow it."

20. In the original Sir James M. Barrie literary classic *Peter Pan*, which of Captain Hook's hands did the hook replace?

21. Complete the line from this song: "This is the night, it's a beautiful night and we call it _____."

22. What Disney character in an animated feature was the first to be named after the actress who provided the voice?

23. How many years did Walt Disney and his staff spend making the full-length animated feature *Sleeping Beauty* (1959)?

24. Walt Disney reportedly enjoyed Eleanor Audley's portrayal of Lady Tremaine in the 1950 animated feature *Cinderella* so much that he personally requested her to return to provide the voice of what other villain?

25. What character is best described by these words in a song?: "If she doesn't scare you, no evil thing will."

26. The song "A Most Befuddling Thing" can be heard in which full-length animated feature?

27. Which of Walt Disney's legendary Nine Old Men was the first to be given the sole directing chore for a full-length animated feature?

28. What was the first animated feature soundtrack to attain gold record status?

29. Actor Tommy Steele, star of Broadway and the Disney film *The Happiest Millionaire* (1967), was originally suggested as the voice of what animated character?

30. Author John Culhane, whose Disney books include *Fantasia 2000: Visions of Hope* and *Aladdin, The Making of an Animated Film*, was used as the inspiration for what 1977 animated character?

31. What kind of animal is Madame Medusa absolutely terrified of in the 1977 full-length animated feature *The Rescuers*?

32. What character from what feature film utters the words, "I'm not a warrior; I'm a pig boy"?

33. Which full-length Disney animated feature includes the largest number of Grammy Award-winning artists, either providing a character voice or contributing to the film's score?

34. From what movie serial actor did Billy Joel admit that he drew his inspiration for his portrayal of Dodger in the 1988 full-length animated feature *Oliver & Company*?

35. Actress Alyssa Milano provided Disney artists with the inspiration for what animated character?

36. Of the four princesses, Snow White, Cinderella, Aurora, and Ariel, which is the only one with brown eyes?

37. Name three of the seven signal relay stations used by the international Rescue Aid Society in the film *The Rescuers Down Under* (1990).

38. What was the first Disney full-length animated feature to gross in its first release more than $100 million in box office receipts domestically?

39. What two full-length animated features premiered in New York City on November 13, fifty-one years apart?

40. According to Disney animator Glen Keane, which character is described as having a gorillalike brow, bridge of the nose like a boar, a mane like a lion, a bear-shaped body, legs and a tail like a wolf, a hind end like a buffalo, and human eyes?

41. What full-length animated feature was known during early production work as "King of the Jungle"?

42. Which character from *The Lion King* (1994) makes the statement, "I was first in line until the little hairball was born"?

43. Which song from the animated feature *The Lion King* (1994) makes references to birth, childhood, loss, youth, romance, adulthood, and rebirth?

44. Which three animated characters were originally going to be called Chaney, Laughton, and Quinn?

45. Academy Award-winning actor Jack Nicholson was first suggested to provide the voice of which Disney villain?

46. What do the animated characters Lumiere and Hades have in common?

47. Which two Disney full-length animated features include the mythical home of the Greek gods, Mount Olympus?

48. The character Scar from the feature *The Lion King* (1994) makes a cameo appearance in what later full-length animated film?

49. How many Academy Award nominations did the film *Hercules* (1997) earn?

50. Which full-length animated feature was the first to be animated almost entirely at the Walt Disney Feature Animation Studios in Florida?

51. What actress who provided a voice in the animated feature *Mulan* (1998) also voiced a character forty-eight years earlier in a Disney film?

52. In 1998, which Disney full-length animated feature was depicted on a U.S. postage stamp?

53. Which modern Disney full-length animated feature was released with international versions of its songs all recorded by the same major artist?

54. During the decade of the 1990s, what was the only year that did not see the release of a Disney full-length animated feature?

55. Which is the only month of the year that has not seen the original release of a Disney full-length animated feature?

Animated Feature Potpourri

Answers:

1. The story "Rip Van Winkle," which was written by Washington Irving and included in his *Sketch Book* (1819), was considered early on by Walt Disney as a full-length animated feature.
2. *Snow White and the Seven Dwarfs* (1937).
3. Walt Disney used the words to describe the evil Queen from *Snow White and the Seven Dwarfs* (1937) when trying to provide his artists with his concept of what the character was to look like.
4. The character Persephone from the 1934 Silly Symphony *The Goddess of Spring* provided Disney animators the opportunity to experiment with animating a human female.
5. Artists applied real rouge to each cel in order to make Snow White appear even more lifelike.
6. True. Early concept drawings featured the Queen as a large, comedic type of character before it was decided to give her a more stately and beautiful look.
7. Four years before the release of Disney's *Snow White and the Seven Dwarfs*, the Max Fleischer Studios released their own version of the story as a short animated cartoon. The part of the Princess was portrayed by Betty Boop.
8. Pierné's musical piece "Cydalise."
9. The animated segment *Rite of Spring* was renamed *A World Is Born* and distributed to schools.
10. *Bambi* (1942) was originally scheduled to be the studio's second release. However, because of the level and degree of realism, the film challenged the animators and therefore production was slowed down.
11. *Saludos Amigos* composers Edward H. Plumb, Paul J. Smith, and Charles Wolcott received the Academy Award nomination for Best Score.
12. *The Three Caballeros* (1945).
13. Peter uses a popgun in an effort to capture the wolf.
14. The Giant kidnapped the Golden Harp because he wanted her to sing him to sleep.
15. Willie the Giant has difficulty saying the word "pistachio."

16. In 1697, author Charles Perrault, collector of the Mother Goose stories, penned the tale of Cinderella, which he included in his book *Tales from Mother Goose*. Perrault's versions of both "Cinderella" and "Sleeping Beauty" were used by Disney in the development of the animated features.

17. The song was written for *Cinderella* (1950) but was never used.

18. *Alice in Wonderland* (1951) with 14 songs.

19. Alice makes the statement after she finds herself lost with no apparent chance of returning home.

20. In the original Barrie play, Captain Hook's hook replaced his right hand. In the 1953 Disney version, the hook replaced the left hand because the change made the animation of tasks, such as writing, easier.

21. "This is the night, it's a beautiful night, and we call it Bella Notte." The song "Bella Notte" was featured in the 1955 full-length animated feature *Lady and the Tramp*.

22. Actress-singer Peggy Lee provided the voice for the character Peg in the 1955 feature *Lady and the Tramp*.

23. According to reports, *Sleeping Beauty* took Walt Disney and his staff ten years to complete. Much of Walt Disney's attention was directed during that time toward the construction of his Disneyland park.

24. In the 1959 animated feature *Sleeping Beauty*, Audley returned to provide the voice of the evil Maleficent.

25. Pongo's pet Roger sings the words that describe the evil Cruella De Vil in a song by Mel Leven from the feature *One Hundred and One Dalmatians* (1961).

26. *The Sword in the Stone* (1963) features the song "A Most Befuddling Thing," written by the Sherman brothers.

27. Wolfgang "Woolie" Reitherman was given the task of directing *The Sword in the Stone* (1963).

28. *The Jungle Book* (1967).

29. Tommy Steele was first suggested for the voice of Robin Hood in the 1973 animated feature by that same name. Actor Brian Bedford eventually provided the voice for the film.

30. A Disney artist spotted Culhane visiting the Disney Studio and decided to use him as the inspiration for the animated character Mr. Snoops in the full-length animated feature *The Rescuers*. He is also caricatured in *Fantasia/2000*.

31. Madame Medusa is terrified of mice.

32. Taran from the 1985 feature *The Black Cauldron*.

33. *Oliver & Company* featured a total of six Grammy Award-winning artists. Voice talents were Billy Joel (Artful Dodger), Bette Midler (Georgette), Cheech Marin (Tito), and Rita Pointer (Rita). Award-winning artists Huey Lewis and Barry Manilow each contributed songs to the film's score.

34. Billy Joel admitted that he drew inspiration from actor Leo Gorcey of *The Dead End Kids* for the voice of Dodger. Joel described Gorcey as the "epitome of a tough kid who deep down was a nice guy," characteristics he described as similar to Dodger's.

35. Actress Alyssa Milano was one of three women used by Disney artist Mark Henn as his inspiration for the character Ariel in *The Little Mermaid* (1989).

36. Snow White is the only one of the four with brown eyes.

37. The seven relay stations are Marshall Islands, Hawaiian Islands, Los Angeles, Denver, St. Louis, Chicago, and Washington, D.C.

38. *Beauty and the Beast* (1991) was the first Disney full-length animated feature to gross in excess of $100 million in domestic box office receipts.

39. On November 13, 1940, *Fantasia* had its world premiere followed fifty-one years later by *Beauty and the Beast* (1991).

40. Glen Keane, who was the supervising animator for the character, was describing Beast from *Beauty and the Beast* (1991). (Glen's father, Bil Keane, is the creator of the *Family Circus* comic strip.)

41. *The Lion King* (1994), during its early production days, was known as "King of the Jungle."

42. The evil Scar makes the statement in reference to Mufasa's son, Simba.

43. The references are all used in the song "Circle of Life."

44. The three names were originally considered for the gargoyles in the 1996 feature *The Hunchback of Notre Dame*. The names were meant to pay tribute to three actors who have over the years played the part of the character Quasimodo in films—Lon Chaney, Charles Laughton, and Anthony Quinn.

45. Actor Jack Nicholson was first suggested for the role of Hades in the 1997 full-length animated feature *Hercules*.

46. They both have flames that come out of their heads and they were both animated by Disney artist Nik Ranieri.

47. The two features that include Mount Olympus are *Fantasia* (1940) and *Hercules* (1997).

48. The character Scar makes a cameo appearance in the 1997 full-length animated feature *Hercules*. Disney artist Andreas Deja was responsible for animating both Scar and Hercules.

49. Two: Best Musical Score and Best Song for "Go the Distance."

50. *Mulan* (1998).

51. Actress June Foray provided the voice of Grandmother Fa in *Mulan* (1998) as well as the voice of Lucifer the cat in *Cinderella* (1950). Over the years, Foray has also provided voices for such Disney films as *Peter Pan* (1953) and *Who Framed Roger Rabbit* (1988). Foray may best be remembered for providing the voice of the non-Disney characters Rocket J. Squirrel and Natasha Fatale on *The Bullwinkle Show* beginning in 1961.

52. In September 1998, the United States Postal Service released a series of stamps honoring significant achievements of the 1930s. A stamp depicting *Snow White and the Seven Dwarfs* (1937) was part of that series.

53. Performer Phil Collins wrote five songs for *Tarzan* (1999) and sings four of them in the film. Collins has also recorded the songs in French, German, Spanish (both Latin American and Castilian), and Italian. This was also the first time Collins has ever recorded songs in these languages. Prior to recording, Collins worked with music and language consultants and learned the words phonetically.

54. The only year of the 1990s that did not see the release of a Disney full-length animated feature was 1993. *The Rescuers Down Under* (1990), *Beauty and the Beast* (1991), *Aladdin* (1992), *The Lion King* (1994), *Pocahontas* (1995), *The Hunchback of Notre Dame* (1996), *Hercules* (1997), *Mulan* (1998), and *Tarzan* (1999).

55. March.

Animation Terminology

Questions:

1. In what California city was the first art gallery to sell Disney animation cels in the 1930s?

2. What was the name of the Disney department developed in the 1930s that consisted of a group of artists whose job it was to design the characters that would be used for upcoming animated films and make sculptures of them?

3. What is the name given to the four-by-eight-foot corkboard animators use on which story sketches are pinned up in order to help them visualize a cartoon's complete story?

4. Why did animators use rotoscoping?

5. What was the name of the camera that was developed in the 1930s which allowed animation art to be filmed in such a way as to create depth and dimension?

6. What do you call the artist who is responsible for the finished paintings that provide the setting for the characters, their action, and, if necessary, any special effects?

7. In the animation process, what is the name of the process for converting the rough and sketchy animation drawings into smooth, clean lines?

8. In making films, what is the name used to describe the viewing of a day's footage of a motion picture that had been processed the previous night in the laboratory?

9. What is the name given to the animator who creates the drawings that occur between the animator's extreme points of a character's action and any other drawings done by an assistant animator?

10. What is the "pencil test" in the animation process?

11. What is the name of the projection machine originally used by animators to view pencil tests?

12. What is the name given to the group of drawings on a sheet of paper that animators use to depict the different views, actions, and attitudes of a character?

13. What is the importance of a work reel?

14. What is a "cel setup"?

15. The Walt Disney Company received the Academy Award in 1992 for the category of Best Scientific or Technical Advancement as a result of what animation technological improvement?

Animation Terminology

1. The Courvoisier Gallery in San Francisco was the first gallery to sell Disney animation art.
2. Character Model Department.
3. The board used by animators became known as a storyboard. The process of using a storyboard to tell a cartoon's complete story in drawings was originated by Walt Disney and his staff in the very early days of the studio.
4. Rotoscoping is a process whereby individual frames of live-action film footage are enlarged and used by animators as a guide to create lifelike movements with their animated characters.
5. The multiplane camera.
6. Background artist.
7. The process is known simply as "cleanup." The cleanup animator will retrace each animation drawing onto a new piece of animation paper.
8. Viewed the next day, the previous day's output is known as "dailies."
9. The animators are known as "in-betweeners."
10. A "pencil test" is the process of photographing frame by frame the rough and cleanup animation drawings for a scene in order to critique the animation for timing and smoothness when the film is projected.
11. Animators used a machine known as a Moviola to view pencil tests.
12. "Model sheets." These model sheets provide a guide for animators to maintain the consistency of a character.
13. A "work reel" provides a working copy of the film, begun by photographing the story sketches on the storyboard along with a "scratch track" of dialogue, effects, and music. These scenes are then spliced together in the proper order to help illustrate the film in rough form from beginning to end. As scenes are animated and finalized, they are cut into the work reel.
14. A "cel setup" consists of a production background, on top of which are laid one or more layers of cels that comprise elements of a specific scene as it would be viewed in one frame of the feature.
15. The company received the Scientific/Technical Academy Award for the development of CAPS. CAPS is an acronym for Computer Animated Production System. CAPS made it possible for the seamless combination of hand-drawn and computer animation, used successfully that year for the film *Beauty and the Beast*.

Disney on Television

Questions:

1. The shows on the original *Disneyland* television series were from what four "realms"?

2. Complete the line, "Who's the leader of the club that's _____."

3. Where did Walt Disney discover Annette Funicello for his *Mickey Mouse Club*?

4. What song from a 1950s Disney television program spent sixteen weeks at the top of the hit parade?

5. A collection of stories written by Johnston McCulley in 1924 provided the inspiration for which Disney television series?

6. What legendary trumpet virtuoso appeared on the 1962 television special *Disneyland After Dark*?

7. Which Mouseketeer later went on to play the part of Wally's girlfriend on one episode of the popular television series *Leave It to Beaver*?

8. The *Wonderful World of Disney* television program *The Magnificent Rebel* was about what classical composer?

9. In the Disney television program *Deacon, the High Noon Dog*, a dog is seen chasing a cat, which inadvertently triggers what famous gunfight?

10. True or false: Disney produced a two-hour television movie about the legendary Bigfoot.

11. What actor played an Elvis impersonator on an episode of *The Golden Girls*?

12. What long-running Touchstone television series' theme song began with the words "Life goes on and so do we"?

13. The popular teenage television series *Saved by the Bell* actually got its start on The Disney Channel. What was the name of the series when it aired on The Disney Channel?

14. How many members of the musical group 'N Sync were featured as Mouseketeers in the 1980s version of the *Mickey Mouse Club*?

15. What is the name of the short-lived Touchstone television game show hosted by Dick Clark?

16. What "heavenly" actress made her screen acting debut in the 1991 television program *Disney Presents: The 100 Lives of Black Jack Savage*?

17. What were Blossom's two brothers' names on the television series by that same name?

18. What Touchstone television series had the working title of *It's All in Your Head*?

19. What is the full name of the Taylor's all-knowing next-door neighbor on the Touchstone television series *Home Improvement*?

20. What type of shirt does Al Borland always wear in the television series *Home Improvement*?

21. What actress played the original "Tool Time Girl" on the television series *Home Improvement*?

22. In the television series *Home Improvement*, Tim's wife, Jill, goes back to college to study what subject?

23. What short-lived 1993 Touchstone television series was about a group of hair stylists?

24. What is the name of the high school Cory Matthews attended in the Touchstone television series *Boy Meets World*?

25. What is the name of Cory's girlfriend in the television series *Boy Meets World*?

26. What is the name of the talking stuffed bunny on the WB television series *Unhappily Ever After*?

27. What type of shop does the character Belle own in the children's television series *Disney's Sing Me a Story: with Belle*?

28. What is the name of The Disney Channel comedy magazine that presented a wacky, witty, and often offbeat look at the people and places of the Walt Disney World Resort?

29. What is the last name of the family in the Touchstone television series *Brotherly Love* and what type of business do they operate?

30. What was the name of the short-lived Touchstone television series starring actress-comedian Lisa Ann Walter about a mother attempting to balance a family life and a career utilizing her newly received law degree?

31. What Touchstone television program made syndication history in November 1996 as the only off-network sitcom ever to rank as the nation's number-one syndicated series?

32. On the Touchstone television series *Soul Man*, who played the part of Pastor Mike Weber?

33. What is the name of Pastor Weber's church in the television series *Soul Man*?

34. What is the name of Pastor Mike Weber's assistant in the television series *Soul Man*?

35. What actor plays the part of Prof. Wayne Szalinski in the television series inspired by the feature film *Honey, I Shrunk the Kids* (1989)?

36. What was the name of the Touchstone television series about a teenage high school student who was killed in a freak accident only to return to Earth to act as his best friend's guardian angel?

37. What is the name of the Award-winning preschool series on The Disney Channel hosted by a seven-foot bear whose nose-to-the-camera style engages children to learn to dance and play with others?

38. What is the title of the animated television series produced by Jumbo Pictures for Disney that is named after a popular children's sandwich?

39. What is the name of The Disney Channel children's series about a family of robots and their life on a robotic planet?

40. What is the name of the people who supposedly live in the realm between television and the Internet on The Disney Channel?

41. What did viewers discover for the first time about the Taylors' all-knowing neighbor in the final episode of *Home Improvement*?

42. What teen pop star known for her song *"...baby one more time"* is a former Mouseketeer?

43. What Disney-released television program stars actress Keri Russell and is about a high school graduate who moves to New York to find romance but ends up finding herself?

44. What young pop star known for her song "Genie in a Bottle" is a former Mouseketeer?

45. What is the name of the Touchstone television series that premiered in 1999 about two divorced parents faced with the difficult task of starting all over?

46. Legendary voice actors June Foray and Bill Scott, best known for providing the voices of Rocky and Bullwinkle, were teamed up again in what Disney animated television series?

47. What Disney animated television series won back-to-back Emmy Awards for Best Daytime Animated Program in 1989 and 1990?

48. What is the name of Goliath and Demona's daughter in the animated television series *Gargoyles*?

49. Unlike the other gargoyles, Demona doesn't change back to stone with the first light of the morning. By day Demona assumes the identity of whom?

50. What is the name of the little killer whale and friend to Ariel in the animated television series *Disney's The Little Mermaid*?

51. *Duck Daze* was the working title for what animated television series?

52. According to the animated television series *Disney's The Mighty Ducks*, what is so special about the goalie mask worn by Wildwing?

53. What is the name of the last surviving Savrian Overlord and nemesis to the Mighty Ducks?

54. What is the name of the team's hulking Zen master?

55. Who is the only one that knows the true identity of the Mighty Ducks?

56. What popular young actor provided the voice of Wildwing in the Disney animated television series *Disney's The Mighty Ducks*?

57. Along with being great hockey players, the Mighty Ducks are also defenders of truth and justice. Where is their cool high-tech command center located?

58. On the animated television series *Disney's Doug*, what are the names of Doug's dog and his best friend who happens to be blue in color?

59. Who is Doug smitten with?

60. Who is the star of Doug's favorite spy movies?

61. What is the name of Doug's favorite rock band and what is the name of the neighborhood bully?

62. What actor provided the voice of Arthur the buzzard on the Disney animated television series *Jungle Cubs*?

63. What is the name of the farm located next to Cruella's manor in the animated television series *One Hundred and One Dalmatians*?

64. *One Saturday Morning* actually represents the address of what?

65. What Disney animated television series follows a quirky group of fourth graders as they share adventures, laughter, and the wonder of self-discovery set against the backdrop of their playground?

66. What is the name of the street-smart leader of the playground gang on the animated television series *Recess*?

67. What is the name of the principal on *Recess* who spends his time scheming and trying to figure out the quickest way to reach his dream; a promotion to a cushy job as principal of the new middle school?

68. What is the name of the cool-as-ice athlete who can do no wrong in the eyes of his playground gang on *Recess*?

69. What Disney animated television series is about a 12-year-old girl and her struggle with adolescence?

70. What 1997 full-length animated feature provided the inspiration for a Disney animated television series?

71. What animated television series holds the record for having more guest appearance voices in its first season than any other program?

72. What is the name of the gym teacher and guidance counselor on *Disney's Hercules*?

73. What familiar Disney character voice can be heard as the voice of Helen of Troy in the animated television series *Disney's Hercules*?

74. What is the name of the school that Hercules and his friends attend in *Disney's Hercules*?

75. What is the name of the animated television series that debuted in 1999 featuring the classic Disney characters Mickey, Minnie, Donald, Goofy, and Pluto?

Disney on Television

Answers:

1. The shows were themed to reflect the exciting adventures that awaited guests when they eventually visited Disneyland park. The four realms were "Fantasyland," "Adventureland," "Frontierland," and "Tomorrowland," just like the lands at the park.
2. "...made for you and me."
3. Walt Disney and *Mickey Mouse Club* producer Bill Walsh discovered future Mouseketeer Annette Funicello at an amateur contest at the Starlight Bowl in Burbank, California.
4. "The Ballad of Davy Crockett" from the *Davy Crockett* television miniseries spent sixteen weeks at the top of the hit parade.
5. Johnston McCulley penned the *Zorro* stories.
6. Music legend Louis Armstrong appeared on the television special *Disneyland After Dark*.
7. Cheryl Holdridge played Julie Foster, Wally's girlfriend, on *Leave It to Beaver* in 1962.
8. *The Magnificent Rebel* told the story of classical composer Ludwig van Beethoven.
9. The two supposedly triggered the famous gunfight at the O.K. Corral.
10. True. The *Bigfoot* television movie was made in 1987.
11. Actor/director Quentin Tarantino played an Elvis impersonator on an episode of *The Golden Girls*.
12. "Life goes on and so do we" is the beginning of the theme song for the Touchstone television series *Empty Nest*.
13. *Good Morning, Miss Bliss*.
14. Two: J. C. Chasez and Justin Timberlake.
15. *The Challengers*.
16. Actress Roma Downey, star of the popular television series *Touched by an Angel*, made her screen debut in *Disney Presents: The 100 Lives of Black Jack Savage*.
17. Blossom's two brothers were Joey and Anthony.
18. *Herman's Head* was originally dubbed *It's All in Your Head*.
19. Wilson Wilson.
20. Al is known for his signature flannel shirts.

21. Pamela Anderson played the role of Lisa, the original "Tool Time Girl." She was followed by Debbie Dunning as Heidi.
22. Jill goes back to college to study psychology.
23. The short-lived television series was known as *Cutters*.
24. Cory and his friends attended John Adams High School.
25. Cory's girlfriend is Topanga, played by actress Danielle Fishel.
26. The stuffed bunny is Mr. Floppy, voiced by actor-comedian Bobcat Goldthwait.
27. In the television series, Belle owns a book-and-music shop.
28. The Disney Channel program was known as *Walt Disney World Inside Out.*
29. The last name of the family is Roman (with the three brothers played by Joey, Matthew, and Andrew Lawrence) and they operate a service garage.
30. The series was known as *Life's Work* and it starred Lisa Ann Walter playing the role of Assistant State's Attorney Lisa Hunter.
31. *Home Improvement.*
32. Dan Aykroyd played widowed Episcopalian minister Mike Weber who is trying to run a congregation as well as care for four rambunctious kids.
33. Pastor Mike Weber's church is St. Steven's Episcopal Church.
34. The bumbling assistant pastor is Father Todd.
35. Actor Peter Scolari plays the part of Prof. Wayne Szalinski on the television series *Honey, I Shrunk the Kids.*
36. *Teen Angel.*
37. *Bear in the Big Blue House.*
38. The animated television series is known as *PB & J Otter*, produced by Jumbo Pictures, in cooperation with The Walt Disney Company.
39. *Rolie Polie Olie.*
40. The Zoogs live in the realm between television and the Internet on The Disney Channel.
41. Wilson, the all-knowing neighbor of the Taylor family, played by actor Earl Hindman, never revealed his full face in the eight seasons the show was on the air. In the show's finale (episode number 201) he finally did.
42. Britney Spears appeared on the *Mickey Mouse Club* on The Disney Channel beginning in 1993.
43. Keri Russell stars in *Felicity*. Russell had been a Mouseketeer in the 1989 version of the *Mickey Mouse Club* as well as Prof. Wayne Szalinski's daughter in *Honey, I Blew Up the Kid* (1992).

44. Christina Aguilera appeared on the *Mickey Mouse Club* on The Disney Channel beginning in 1993.

45. The series is known as *Once and Again*. It stars actor Billy Campbell, who had played the Rocketeer in the 1991 Disney film by that same name.

46. The two worked together on *Disney's Adventures of the Gummi Bears*.

47. *The New Adventures of Winnie the Pooh* captured two consecutive Emmy Awards beginning in 1989.

48. Angela is the daughter of Goliath and Demona who attempts to change her mother's evil ways.

49. By day, Demona assumes the identity of Dominique Destine, CEO of a high-tech corporation named Nightstone whose sole objective is to destroy the human species.

50. The innocent little whale is Spot.

51. *Quack Pack*.

52. The mask worn by Mighty Ducks goalie Wildwing was originally developed by duck warrior Drake DuCaine to help defend his planet from the evil Savrian Overlords. The mask gave Wildwing special powers of reason and insight along with confidence and courage.

53. Lord Dragaunus is the last surviving Savrian Overlord. The Mighty Ducks look to defend Earth from the evil Lord Dragaunus, who resembles a dinosaur and dragon, with a voice provided by actor Tim Curry.

54. The team's Zen master is Grin, voiced by actor Brad Garrett. Garrett may best be known for his recurring role on the television comedy *Everybody Loves Raymond* playing the role of brother Robert Barone.

55. The only individual who knows the true identity of the Mighty Ducks is their manager Phil, voiced by actor Jim Belushi.

56. Actor Ian Ziering, star of *Beverly Hills 90210*, provided the voice of the animated Wildwing.

57. The Mighty Ducks command center is located below the hockey rink's ice. The facility is known as the Ready Room and it features a super-computer known as Drake One.

58. Doug's dog is Porkchop and his blue friend is Skeeter. Fred Newman provides the voice of both characters. Interestingly, Newman was also the host of the *Mickey Mouse Club* for six seasons starting when it debuted in 1989.

59. Doug has the biggest crush on Patti Mayonnaise.

60. Doug's favorite spy movie star is Smash Adams.

61. Doug's favorite rock band is The Beets and the bully is Roger Klotz.

62. Actor David Lander provided the voice of Arthur the buzzard in the animated series *Disney's Jungle Cubs*. Lander may best be remembered for his portrayal of the character Andrew "Squiggy" Squiggman on the television series *Laverne & Shirley* (1976–1983).

63. Dearly Farm.

64. *Disney's One Saturday Morning* is actually a reference to the address of the virtual building where "everything about Saturday" is created. The program utilizes the largest virtual set ever created for television.

65. *Disney's Recess.*

66. The popular street-smart leader and consummate prankster of the group is T. J. Detweiler. The character's voice is provided by Andrew Lawrence, youngest of the Lawrence brothers.

67. Principal Prickley voiced by Dabney Coleman.

68. The playground's athlete is Vince.

69. *Disney's Pepper Ann.*

70. The animated feature *Hercules* provides the basis for the animated television series *Disney's Hercules*, which premiered in 1998. The animated television series, a spin-off from the feature film, follows Hercules during his formative adolescent high school and hero-in-training years.

71. During its first season, *Disney's Hercules* had a cast of over 160 voices. Some of the guest voices include Merv Griffin, Heather Locklear, Kathie Lee Gifford, William Shatner, and Wayne Newton.

72. The gym teacher is Phys Oedipus, voiced by fitness guru Richard Simmons, and the guidance counselor is Parenthesis, who is voiced by actor Eric Idle with dialogue appropriately peppered with parenthetical phrases.

73. Actress Jodi Benson provides the voice of Helen of Troy in *Disney's Hercules*. Benson may best be remembered for providing the voice of Ariel in the animated feature *The Little Mermaid* (1989).

74. Prometheus Academy.

75. *Mickey's MouseWorks* premiered on May 1, 1999, as part of the ABC network's top-rated Saturday morning lineup. The half-hour series features new cartoons that range in length from ninety seconds to twelve minutes featuring Mickey, Minnie, Donald, Goofy, and Pluto.

Made-for-Video Films

Questions:

1. What is the name of the first Disney animated movie created exclusively for video?

2. What is the name of the clumsy thief who inadvertently releases Jafar from the magic lamp?

3. What is the name of the made-for-video sequel to the *Honey, I Shrunk the Kids* film series?

4. In *Pooh's Grand Adventure: The Search for Christopher Robin* (1997), where has Christopher Robin actually gone off to?

5. What is the name of the made-for-video film that tells the story of how Belle celebrated Christmas while imprisoned in the Beast's castle?

6. What is the name of the evil pipe organ that plots to keep the Beast from falling in love with Belle?

7. What was the first movie produced by the Walt Disney animation studios in Canada?

8. In *The Lion King II: Simba's Pride* (1998), what is the name of Simba and Nala's daughter?

9. What actress provides the voice of the evil Zira in *The Lion King II: Simba's Pride* (1998)?

10. In *The Lion King II: Simba's Pride*, what is the name of Scar's apparent handpicked successor?

11. What is the name of the 1998 made-for-video sequel to the animated feature *Pocahontas* (1995)?

12. What actor provided the voice of Captain John Smith in the made-for-video sequel to the animated feature *Pocahontas*?

13. What is the name of the 1999 made-for-video live-action comedy film based on a story by Ray Bradbury?

14. What is the name of the made-for-video film based on the 1997 animated feature *Hercules*?

15. What is the name of the made-for-video feature film starring Mickey Mouse celebrating the Christmas holiday season?

Made-for-Video Films

Answers:

1. The first Disney animated movie created exclusively for video was *The Return of Jafar* which was released on May 20, 1994. The made-for-video sequel to *Aladdin* (1992) picks up where the feature left off with the evil Jafar inside a magic lamp.
2. The thief who releases the now powerful Jafar is Abis Mal.
3. The made-for-video film is *Honey, We Shrunk Ourselves* (1997). This time Prof. Wayne Szalinski has to deal with the government, which has placed a ban on his amazing shrinking device. Before the machine can be shipped off to the Smithsonian Institution he turns the device on one more time and accidentally points it at himself.
4. Christopher Robin is missing and the characters from the Hundred-Acre Wood organize a journey to find him. Though Pooh and friends do not know it, Christopher Robin is not missing but rather is off to school.
5. *Beauty and the Beast: The Enchanted Christmas* (1997).
6. The evil pipe organ is Forte, voiced by Tim Curry.
7. Walt Disney Animation Canada studios in Vancouver and Toronto first produced *Beauty and the Beast: The Enchanted Christmas* (1997).
8. Simba and Nala's daughter is Kiara.
9. Actress Suzanne Pleshette provides the voice of the evil Zira. Pleshette has also appeared in such Disney films as *The Ugly Dachshund* (1966), *The Adventures of Bullwhip Griffin* (1967), *Blackbeard's Ghost* (1968), and *The Shaggy D.A.* (1976).
10. Kovu.
11. *Pocahontas II: Journey to a New World*. In the film, Pocahontas travels to England and discovers a land unlike anything she has ever experienced.
12. The role of Captain John Smith was voiced by Donal Gibson, younger brother of Mel Gibson, who had provided the voice of the character in the original animated feature.

13. Ray Bradbury's story "The Magic White Suit," which appeared in a 1957 issue of *The Saturday Evening Post*, provided the basis for the film *The Wonderful Ice Cream Suit*. The film tells the story of five men, each down on their luck with only $100 between them, who buy a magical white suit that ultimately changes their lives. The film was used to celebrate and raise funds for the New Mexico Hispanic Cultural Center in Albuquerque.

14. *Hercules: Zero to Hero* (1999).

15. *Mickey's Once Upon a Christmas* (1999).

Live-Action Films

Questions:

1. Why do Sir Giles and the dragon stage a mock fight in the 1941 Disney feature *The Reluctant Dragon*?

2. What actor served as the narrator of the *Baby Weems* animated segment in *The Reluctant Dragon*?

3. What was the first Disney film to have its world premiere in Atlanta, Georgia?

4. How many tales about Brer Rabbit does Uncle Remus tell Johnny in *Song of the South* (1946)?

5. What Disney film was photographed entirely on the Pribilof Islands off the coast of Alaska?

6. What became of the film footage featuring Eskimos after it was edited out of the footage that became the 1948 nature film *Seal Island*?

7. How many Mouseketeers appeared in the motion picture *Westward Ho the Wagons!* (1956)—none, two, four, or six?

8. What Disney film includes two train locomotives named the *Texas* and the *General*?

9. What film's last line is "What do you mean you got a dog? We've got a dog!"

10. What late actor made his Disney debut playing the part of William "Bill" Dunn in the 1960 film *Ten Who Dared*?

11. What continent provided the setting for the True-Life Adventure film *Jungle Cat* (1960)?

12. What is the title of the 1960 featurette about a dog named Nubbin who is raised by a raccoon?

13. Which Mouseketeer accepted on behalf of Hayley Mills her Academy Award for Best Performance by a Juvenile in 1960?

14. What two Disney films were based on books by German author Erich Kastner?

15. What 1961 Disney musical motion picture was originally proposed as a full-length animated feature?

16. What Disney film features vocal performances by both Annette Funicello and Hayley Mills?

17. How many Disney feature films include music of the Sherman brothers—5, 8, 16, or 28?

18. Nikki, featured in the film *Nikki, Wild Dog of the North* (1961), gets washed down river with what kind of animal?

19. The songs "Merci Beaucoup" and "Grimpons!" were both featured in which 1962 Disney film?

20. What is the first Disney film that had an outer space theme?

21. What Disney film includes the beautiful song, "Just Say Auf Wiedersehen"?

22. In how many Disney films were Tommy Kirk and Kevin Corcoran featured as brothers?

23. In the 1963 Disney film *The Incredible Journey*, what becomes of the pets' owners that causes the pets to journey across two hundred miles of Canadian wilderness?

24. In the 1963 feature *Savage Sam*, how does the search party eventually locate Travis, Arliss, and Lisbeth?

25. The book *Mother Carey's Chickens*, written by Kate Douglas Wiggin, provided the inspiration for which 1963 Disney film?

26. During the filming of what 1960s Disney film did a tiger get loose on the studio lot?

27. What film's soundtrack was Disney's first number one album on the *Billboard* charts?

28. What Disney motion picture accomplished the rare feat of earning a husband and wife an Academy Award nomination each in different categories for the same film?

29. Actress Betty Lou Gerson, voice of the animated character Cruella De Vil in *101 Dalmatians*, made a cameo appearance in what 1964 feature film?

30. What 1965 Disney film was based on a book entitled *Undercover Cat*?

31. For what Disney film were live olive trees planted on the Disney studio back lot?

32. What is the last name of the family in the 1968 Disney feature *The One and Only, Genuine, Original Family Band*?

33. Who directed *Never a Dull Moment* (1968) and what connection does he have to the film's star?

34. What 1969 Disney film had a working title of *Boy-Car-Girl*?

35. What is the name of the fictitious broadcasting company depicted in the film *The Barefoot Executive* (1971)?

36. Actor John Ritter made his motion picture debut in what 1971 Disney film?

37. Actresses Lynn Redgrave, Leslie Caron, and Judy Carne were all at one point considered for what character in the 1971 feature *Bedknobs and Broomsticks*?

38. What popular actor who starred in the television series *St. Elsewhere* made his screen debut in the 1972 Disney film *Now You See Him, Now You Don't*?

39. How many Disney films starred actor Fred MacMurray?

40. What Disney film set in Hawaii was originally referred to by its working title, *Paniolo*?

41. What kind of dog does "Honest John" Slade, played by Disney regular Keenan Wynn, get transformed into at the conclusion of the film *The Shaggy D.A.* (1976)?

42. Location scenes featuring a Maine coastal town's lighthouse in the 1977 feature *Pete's Dragon* were actually filmed where?

43. In *Herbie Goes to Monte Carlo* (1977), what two cities serve as the start and finish of the big race?

44. What is the name of the Earth cat Jake falls in love with in the film *The Cat from Outer Space* (1978)?

45. What is the name of the big race in which Herbie competes during the 1980 Disney film *Herbie Goes Bananas*?

46. The first full-length motion picture to feature extensive use of computer imagery was a 1982 Disney film. What was its title?

47. What 1985 Disney film was considered by audiences a sequel to a 1939 MGM film?

48. Name the two Disney feature films that include a character named Gideon.

49. What is the last name of the character Ernest in the film series that stars actor Jim Varney?

50. Name two of three Disney feature films that were partially filmed in Norway.

51. Who is the only actor to have starred in at least one Disney feature film during the 1960s, '70s, '80s, and '90s?

52. In the live-action version of *The Jungle Book* (1994), what causes Mowgli to be separated from his father?

53. What identity does the boy Preston Waters assume in the 1994 Disney film *Blank Check*?

54. What is the name of the head angel in the 1994 Disney film *Angels in the Outfield*?

55. What 1995 Disney film tells the story of five Green Berets stationed in Vietnam in 1968 who undertake a secret mission to transport an 8,000-pound prized elephant through three hundred miles of rugged terrain?

56. In the 1995 Disney film *Tall Tale*, with what two other legendary figures does Pecos Bill team up to help save the town of Paradise Valley from a band of ruthless speculators?

57. What popular actor played Pecos Bill in the Disney film *Tall Tale* (1995)?

58. What Disney film tells the story of a straight-laced lawyer who seeks the affection of a single mother only to realize he has to walk on eggshells because of her eleven-year-old son, Ben?

59. Name two of the three 1995 Disney-released films to receive Academy Award nominations in the category of Best Original Musical or Comedy Score?

60. What is the name of the camp for overweight children in the 1995 motion picture *Heavyweights*?

61. Actor Emilio Estevez agreed to appear in the Disney film *D3: The Mighty Ducks* (1996) if, instead of receiving a salary, the studio would help finance which motion picture that he wanted to direct?

62. What two characters do Kermit the Frog and Miss Piggy portray in the feature *Muppet Treasure Island* (1996)?

63. In the classic book *Treasure Island*, the character Long John Silver was portrayed as having a parrot perched on his shoulder. In *Muppet Treasure Island* (1996), instead of a parrot, what did Long John Silver have on his shoulder?

64. What three Disney feature films include characters that are genies?

65. What is the name of the Disney film that tells the story of twelve-year-old Josh Framm and the challenges of life he faces with the help of his dog, who has a talent for basketball?

66. In the 1997 remake of the motion picture *That Darn Cat*, what actress portrayed the role originated by Hayley Mills?

67. What Disney film tells the story of New York City commodities trader Michael Cromwell, who has to travel to the deepest areas of the Amazon in order to get his estranged wife's signature on a divorce decree so that he can remarry?

68. How many Disney films included actor Dean Jones—5, 9 11, or 15?

69. Which 1997 Disney film tells that story of computer nerd Fred Z. Randall, who is recruited to become a replacement astronaut in the first-ever manned mission to the planet Mars?

70. Name three Disney feature films that include the word "jungle" in the title.

71. What 1998 Disney film is loosely based on Aesop's fable "The Ant and the Grasshopper"?

72. Academy Award-winning actor Robert De Niro was originally considered for what unsavory character in the 1998 film *A Bug's Life*?

73. What 1999 Disney film is about an ambitious journalist who thinks he has stumbled on the story of the century when he discovers a real-life Martian whose spacecraft has crash-landed on Earth?

74. What 1999 adventure comedy is about a naive and inept security guard named John Brown, who is literally blown to pieces by the evil Dr. Claw only to be reconstructed again by scientist Brenda Bradford?

75. What 1999 Disney Pictures film tells the true-life story of courage and triumph of Ethiopian long-distance runner Haile Gebrselassie?

76. What 1986 Touchstone Pictures release was inspired by an early Jean Renoir film titled *Boudu Saved from Drowning*?

77. What popular actor made his screen acting debut in the 1986 Touchstone film *Ruthless People*?

78. Who accepted the Academy Award for Best Actor on behalf of Paul Newman, who won for his role in the 1986 feature *The Color of Money*?

79. What 1987 Touchstone Pictures film was adapted from the French motion picture *Trois Hommes et un Couffin*?

80. On the set of which 1988 Touchstone Pictures film did Meg Ryan and future husband Dennis Quaid meet?

81. In what city did *Who Framed Roger Rabbit* (1988) have its world premiere?

82. What kind of animals serve as the backup singers for Jessica Rabbit when she performs at the Ink & Paint Club in *Who Framed Roger Rabbit*?

83. Which two characters square off in a dueling piano competition at the Ink & Paint Club in *Who Framed Roger Rabbit*?

84. In *Who Framed Roger Rabbit*, who does Eddie Valiant confuse with Jessica Rabbit when he travels to Toontown?

85. What popular actor played the part of Brian Flanagan, the flashy bartender who becomes a star of the club circuit in the 1988 feature *Cocktail*?

86. Prior to the 1997 release of the Hollywood Pictures film *G.I. Jane*, which 1988 Touchstone film also dealt with the Navy SEALS?

87. Actress Bette Midler sings which song from *Dumbo* in the motion picture *Beaches* (1988)?

88. What 1988 Touchstone Pictures film received a Grammy Award for Best Song and Best Record?

89. What was the first Touchstone Pictures film to receive an Academy Award nomination for Best Picture?

90. What 1990 Touchstone Pictures film received an Academy Award nomination for its female lead for Best Actress?

91. What popular actor plays Mr. Destiny, the mysterious man with unique powers, in the 1990 film by that same name?

92. What 1991 Touchstone film stars Gérard Depardieu and Andie MacDowell, who arrange a marriage of convenience?

93. What is the name of the book written by Dr. Leo Marvin in the 1991 film *What About Bob?*

94. What is the name of the New Hampshire lakefront vacation destination featured in the 1991 film *What About Bob?*

95. What Touchstone Pictures film had a working title of *The Mrs.*?

96. Which 1964 Mary Wells song had its words and title changed to "My God" for *Sister Act?*

97. At the conclusion of the film *Sister Act* (1992) the nuns give a special concert performance for what distinguished visitor?

98. What 1994 Touchstone Pictures film was originally dubbed in early film screenings as *By the Book?*

99. In the 1994 film *Renaissance Man* actor Danny DeVito plays marketing executive Bill Rago, who is forced to teach a group of military misfits. What classic story helps Rago get his class excited about learning?

100. Prior to the film *George of the Jungle* (1997), what was the last Disney film to feature actor Brendan Fraser?

101. What 1994 film was inspired by a skit that appeared on the popular *Saturday Night Live* television program?

102. What 1994 Touchstone film was written and produced by Steve Martin?

103. What is the name of the television morning show that Ellen DeGeneres works for in the 1996 Touchstone film *Mr. Wrong*?

104. What 1996 Touchstone Pictures film tells the story of a small-town weather reporter who lands a position as a prime-time anchor only to have a romance with the station's veteran news anchor?

105. What 1996 film stars John Travolta playing the part of George Malley, a regular guy whose life is turned upside down after he is struck by a blinding white light on his 37th birthday?

106. What is the name of the company owned by airline mogul Tom Mullen in the film *Ransom* (1996)?

107. What is the name of the young actor who played kidnap victim Sean Mullen in the film *Ransom* (1996)?

108. The film *The Preacher's Wife* is a remake of which 1947 MGM motion picture?

109. What character does Denzel Washington play in the 1996 film *The Preacher's Wife*?

110. What 1997 film stars Academy Award-winning actor Nicolas Cage as a prison parolee who discovers himself embroiled in a midair hijacking of a plane filled with some of the nation's most dangerous criminals?

111. What 1997 Touchstone Pictures film received an Academy Award nomination for Best Song?

112. What 1998 Touchstone Pictures film stars actor Robert Redford as a man who has the unique ability of talking to horses?

113. What 1998 Touchstone Pictures film stars Harrison Ford as Quinn Harris, a rough-hewn aviator living an uncomplicated existence in paradise until he meets Robin Monroe, played by actress Anne Heche, a sharp New York City magazine editor on vacation?

114. What 1998 Touchstone Pictures film stars Adam Sandler and is about a backwoods thirty-one-year-old lovable loser from Louisiana who becomes the winning ticket for a struggling college football team?

115. What 1998 Touchstone film is based on a Pulitzer Prize-winning novel by Toni Morrison about a woman whose path to freedom is obstructed by haunting secrets of her past?

116. What 1998 Touchstone Pictures film tells the story of attorney Robert Clayton Dean who finds himself unknowingly in a situation which pits him against the National Security Agency and a web of deceit and crime?

117. What 1998 Touchstone Pictures comedy film is about a quirky and precocious tenth-grade student named Max Fischer and his pursuit to win over a teacher's heart?

118. Which 1998 Touchstone Pictures film became the top-grossing live-action motion picture of any studio released in that year?

119. What was the name of the 1999 courtroom thriller starring John Travolta and Robert Duvall about the actual events surrounding a legal crusade on behalf of eight families in Massachusetts against several corporations that contaminated the town's drinking water?

120. What 1999 Touchstone Pictures film was inspired by Shakespeare's *Taming of the Shrew,* and tells the story of two sisters, the popular Bianca and the ill-tempered Kat?

121. What 1999 Touchstone Pictures film tells the story of an ambitious psychiatrist who attempts to unlock the deep-seated mystery within the mind of a brilliant imprisoned primatologist?

122. What 1999 Touchstone Pictures film is based on Michael Crichton's best-selling novel *Eaters of the Dead?*

123. What 1999 Touchstone Pictures film is based on a story by Isaac Asimov about an ageless android named Andrew Martin who spends two hundred years becoming human?

124. Which Academy Award-winning composer provided the music for the film *Bicentennial Man* (1999)?

125. What 2000 Touchstone Pictures film's title is the same as a previous Disney park attraction?

126. What symbol is used as the logo for Hollywood Pictures?

127. What popular actor plays the part of the exterminator in the 1990 Hollywood Pictures film *Arachnophobia*?

128. What 1991 film tells the story of law student Charlie Farrow who accidentally kills the son of a notorious mobster and is then forced to flee for his life?

129. What two actors who starred in the 1992 film *Straight Talk* also provided voices for two Disney animated characters?

130. Besides *The Little Mermaid* (1989), what other Disney feature film includes a character named Ariel?

131. What is the name of Eddie Murphy's character in the 1992 film *The Distinguished Gentleman*?

132. What public office does Eddie Murphy's character run for in *The Distinguished Gentleman*?

133. What popular star of the NBC television series *ER* played a Nazi in the 1993 film *Swing Kids*?

134. Actress Ming-Na Wen, who appeared in *The Joy Luck Club* (1993), later went on to provide the voice of which Disney animated character?

135. What legendary actor plays the part of the rancher named Hooker in the motion picture *Tombstone* (1993)?

136. What was the first Hollywood Pictures film to receive an Academy Award nomination for Best Picture?

137. Which Academy Award–winning composer provided the music for the Hollywood Pictures film *Nixon* (1995)?

138. Actor Antonio Banderas and actress Melanie Griffith first met on the set of which 1995 Hollywood Pictures film?

139. What 1996 Hollywood Pictures film retells the true-life story of thirteen prep school students and the traumatic events surrounding an expedition aboard the sailing ship *Albatross* in the Caribbean?

140. What Hollywood Pictures film stars Dan Aykroyd and Daniel Stern as two die-hard Boston Celtic basketball fans who kidnap an opposing team's obnoxious superstar during the NBA Championship?

141. Who directed the 1996 Hollywood Pictures film *Jack*?

142. What 1996 Hollywood Pictures film won the Academy Award for Best Song?

143. What popular actor portrays the narrator, the revolutionary leader Ché Guevara, in the film *Evita* (1996)?

144. What city was used for the filming of the funeral procession of Eva Perón in *Evita* (1996)?

145. What major actor in the film *Evita* (1996) plays a character whose initials are the same as his own?

146. What is the name of the 1997 Hollywood Pictures film that tells the story of Martin, a professional assassin, who returns home so he can attend his ten-year high school reunion?

147. What 1997 film had a working title of *In Pursuit of Honor*?

148. What actor provides the narration and portrays the role of the grown-up, Joe, in the 1998 Hollywood Picture film *Simon Birch*?

149. What 1999 suspense thriller stars Bruce Willis playing the part of a child psychologist and the eerie encounters he has with a young boy named Cole Sear, who has the ability to see dead people?

150. What 1999 Hollywood Pictures film stars Russell Crowe and Burt Reynolds and is about an amateur hockey team that agrees to play the New York Rangers professional hockey team?

Live-Action Films

Answers:

1. The townspeople requested the great Sir Giles to rid their village of the fierce dragon. However, Sir Giles and the dragon, having become friends, were reluctant to do battle and preferred to have tea. They staged the fight so as not to disappoint the townspeople.
2. Alan Ladd.
3. On November 12, 1946, *Song of the South* had its world premiere in Atlanta, Georgia. The city was the home of author Joel Chandler Harris, upon whose writings the film was based.
4. Three.
5. *Seal Island* (1948).
6. The edited footage was used to produce an entirely new film *The Alaskan Eskimo* (1953). Both films received Academy Awards in Short Subject categories.
7. The film became an ideal way to help promote the Mouseketeers, who were simultaneously appearing in the popular television series the *Mickey Mouse Club*. The film featured four Mouseketeers: Doreen Tracey, Carl "Cubby" O'Brien, Tommy Cole, and Karen Pendleton. In addition, the film also featured David Stollery, star of the *Mickey Mouse Club* serial *The Adventures of Spin and Marty*.
8. The two classic locomotives appeared in the 1956 Disney film, *The Great Locomotive Chase*.
9. *The Shaggy Dog* (1959).
10. Actor Brian Keith made his Disney debut in *Ten Who Dared* (1960). Keith went on to become a regular, appearing in six other Disney motion pictures: *The Parent Trap* (1961), *Moon Pilot* (1962), *Savage Sam* (1963), *A Tiger Walks* (1964), *Those Calloways* (1965), and *Scandalous John* (1971).
11. South America.
12. *The Hound That Thought He Was a Raccoon.*
13. Actress Annette Funicello accepted the award on behalf of Hayley Mills. The award was presented to Funicello by Shirley Temple.
14. *The Parent Trap* (1961) and *Emil and the Detectives* (1964).
15. *Babes in Toyland.*
16. *The Parent Trap* (1961) features performances by Annette Funicello and Hayley Mills. Funicello and Tommy Sands sang the film's title song, "The Parent Trap," and Mills sang the song "Let's Get Together" when

she portrayed the characters of both Susan and Sharon.

17. Remarkably, twenty-eight Disney films have included songs by the Sherman brothers. Their first work for Disney was for the 1961 film *The Absent-Minded Professor* and most recently for *The Tigger Movie* in 2000.

18. A bear.

19. *In Search of the Castaways.*

20. *Moon Pilot* (1962).

21. *Miracle of the White Stallions* (1963).

22. The two actually appeared as brothers in five different Disney films; *Old Yeller* (1957), *The Shaggy Dog* (1959), *Swiss Family Robinson* (1960), *Bon Voyage* (1962), and *Savage Sam* (1963).

23. The three pets, two dogs and a cat, thought they had been abandoned but in reality their owners had taken a trip to Europe and left them with friends.

24. The three were kidnapped by an Indian tribe and it took Savage Sam and his keen sense of smell to find them.

25. The book *Mother Carey's Chickens* provided the inspiration for *Summer Magic.*

26. During the filming of the 1964 feature *A Tiger Walks*, a tiger got loose for a short time on the studio lot.

27. *Mary Poppins* (1964).

28. Tony Walton received an Academy Award nomination for Best Costume Design and his wife at that time, Julie Andrews, was nominated for and received the award for Best Actress for the 1964 feature *Mary Poppins.*

29. Actress Betty Lou Gerson made a cameo appearance as an old crone in the film *Mary Poppins* (1964).

30. *Undercover Cat* provided the inspiration for the 1965 feature *That Darn Cat.* The book's authors were known as the Gordons.

31. *Monkeys, Go Home!* (1967).

32. The family's name is Bower and they represented eleven members of the band.

33. *Never a Dull Moment* was directed by Jerry Paris and the film starred actor Dick Van Dyke. Paris and Van Dyke were neighbors on the Emmy Award-winning 1960s comedy series *The Dick Van Dyke Show* (1961–1966).

34. *The Love Bug* was originally referred to as "Boy-Car-Girl."

35. The fictitious broadcasting company is known as UBC (United Broadcasting Corporation). Its logo combines elements of the three largest television networks and their symbols at that time: NBC's peacock feather, ABC's small caption, and CBS's eye.

36. John Ritter made his screen acting debut in *The Barefoot Executive*. Ritter may best be remembered for playing the part of Jack Tripper in the television comedy *Three's Company* (1977–1984).

37. All three actresses were at one point considered for the part of Eglantine Price in *Bedknobs and Broomsticks*.

38. Ed Begley Jr. made his screen debut in the 1972 film *Now You See Him, Now You Don't*. Begley went on to appear in several other Disney comedy films such as *Superdad* (1973), *Charley and the Angel* (1973), and *Renaissance Man* (1994).

39. Seven; *The Shaggy Dog* (1959), *The Absent-Minded Professor* (1961), *Bon Voyage* (1962), *Son of Flubber* (1963), *Follow Me, Boys!* (1966), *The Happiest Millionaire* (1967), and *Charley and the Angel* (1973).

40. The 1974 Disney film *The Castaway Cowboy* was originally referred to by the Polynesian name for "cowboy," which is Paniolo.

41. The scandalous Slade is transformed into a bulldog at the conclusion of the film.

42. Location scenes depicting a Maine lighthouse were actually shot in Morro Bay, California.

43. The race is from Paris to Monte Carlo.

44. Jake falls in love with Lucy Belle.

45. The big race is known as the Grande Premio do Brasil.

46. *Tron.*

47. *Return to Oz* (1985) was considered the sequel to the 1939 MGM motion picture *The Wizard of Oz*.

48. Honest John's accomplice is Gideon in *Pinocchio* and actor Harry Dean Stanton plays an angel named Gideon in *One Magic Christmas* (1985).

49. Ernest's last name is Worrell.

50. *The Island at the Top of the World* (1974), *Flight of the Navigator* (1986), and *Shipwrecked* (1991).

51. Actor Kurt Russell has starred in at least one film in each of those decades.

52. The tiger Shere Khan killed Mowgli's father, leaving Mowgli no other choice but to find shelter and protection in the jungle.

53. Preston Waters, played by actor Brian Bonsall, takes the name Macintosh so that he can freely spend the money he has received from the gangster who accidentally gives him a blank check. The young Preston took the name after seeing the name Macintosh on his computer. Bonsall may best be remembered for playing the role of Andrew in the 1980s television series *Family Ties*.

54. The head angel is Al, played by actor Christopher Lloyd.

55. *Operation Dumbo Drop*. In the film, Captain Sam Cahill, played by actor Danny Glover, agrees to transport a sacred elephant to the village of Montagnard in Dak Nhe for a ceremonial ritual.

56. Bill is aided by Paul Bunyan and John Henry in saving the town of Paradise Valley.

57. Patrick Swayze.

58. *Man of the House* (1995).

59. The three films *Pocahontas*, *Toy Story*, and *Unstrung Heroes*.

60. Camp Hope.

61. *The War at Home*.

62. Kermit the Frog portrays the ship's captain, Smollett, and Miss Piggy plays the part of Benjamina. The latter character in the Robert Louis Stevenson literary classic *Treasure Island* was known as Ben Gunn.

63. In *Muppet Treasure Island* the character Long John Silver had a lobster on his shoulder.

64. *Ducktales: The Movie, Treasure of the Lost Lamp* (1990), *Aladdin* (1992), and *Kazaam* (1996).

65. The name of the film is *Air Bud* (1997).

66. Actress Christina Ricci played the part of Patti Randall in *That Darn Cat*.

67. *Jungle 2 Jungle* (1997). In the film, Cromwell, played by actor Tim Allen, discovers he has a thirteen-year-old son who is being raised in the jungle.

68. Dean Jones is one of Disney's most prolific actors, appearing in nine motion pictures: *That Darn Cat* (1965), *The Ugly Dachshund* (1966), *Monkeys, Go Home!* (1967), *Blackbeard's Ghost* (1968), *The Horse in the Gray Flannel Suit* (1968), *Million Dollar Duck* (1971), *Snowball Express* (1972), *The Shaggy D.A.* (1976), and *That Darn Cat* (1997).

69. *RocketMan*.

70. *Jungle Cat* (1960), *The Jungle Book* (1967), *Rudyard Kipling's The Jungle Book* (1994), *Jungle 2 Jungle* (1997), and *George of the Jungle* (1997).

71. *A Bug's Life*.

72. Robert De Niro was originally considered for the voice of Hopper in the 1998 feature *A Bug's Life.*

73. *My Favorite Martian.* In the film, the Martian takes human form and poses as Tim's Uncle Martin. Tim eventually helps Martin in getting his spacecraft repaired so that he can return to his home planet.

74. The 1999 film is *Inspector Gadget,* starring actor Matthew Broderick, with scientist Brenda Bradford played by Joely Fisher. In the film, Bradford rebuilds the poor security guard, equipping him with many accessories and talents.

75. The film is *Endurance,* and it tells the true-life story of Ethiopian runner Haile Gebrselassie and the legendary 10,000-meter race he ran at the 1996 Olympic Summer Games in Atlanta, Georgia.

76. *Down and Out in Beverly Hills.*

77. Actor Bill Pullman, star of such films as *While You Were Sleeping* (1995) and *Independence Day* (1996), made his screen acting debut in *Ruthless People.*

78. Academy Award-winning director Robert Wise accepted the award on behalf of Paul Newman. The award was presented by legendary actress Bette Davis.

79. *Three Men and a Baby.*

80. Meg Ryan and Dennis Quaid costarred in the Touchstone Pictures thriller *D.O.A.*

81. *Who Framed Roger Rabbit* had its world premiere at New York City's famed Radio City Music Hall.

82. Jessica's backup singers are the crows from *Dumbo.*

83. Donald Duck competes with Warner Brothers cartoon character Daffy Duck.

84. The character's name is Lena Hyena.

85. Tom Cruise plays the part of Brian Flanagan, who returns from military service to begin a new career in civilian life as a bartender in the film *Cocktail.* Cruise spent weeks at bartending school to help develop the skills he needed for the role.

86. *The Rescue* featured the Navy SEALS.

87. Bette Midler sings the song "Baby Mine" in the film *Beaches.*

88. *Beaches.* The Grammy Award for Best Song went to Larry Henley and Jeff Silbar and the award for Best Record went to Bette Midler for the song "Wind Beneath My Wings."

89. *Dead Poets Society* (1989).

90. Julia Roberts received the nomination for *Pretty Woman.*

91. Mr. Destiny is played by actor Michael Caine.

92. *Green Card.* Depardieu's character wants the marriage so he can stay in the United States and MacDowell's character must participate in the agreement in order for her to rent an apartment.

93. Dr. Leo Marvin's book is entitled *Baby Steps.*

94. Lake Winnipesaukee.

95. *The Mrs.* was the original name for the 1991 Touchstone Pictures film *Deceived.*

96. The sisters change the words to the classic 1964 Mary Wells song from "My Guy" to "My God."

97. The sisters put on a special concert performance for Pope John Paul II.

98. *Renaissance Man.*

99. The group is excited after hearing dialogue from Shakespeare's *Hamlet.*

100. Brendan Fraser made a cameo appearance in the 1994 Touchstone Pictures film *In the Army Now.* Fraser played the character Link, a reference to the character he played in the 1992 Hollywood Pictures film *Encino Man.*

101. *It's Pat.*

102. *A Simple Twist of Faith* was written by, produced by, and starred Steve Martin.

103. Ellen DeGeneres plays the part of Martha Alston and she works on the fictitious television show *Daybreak San Diego* on KSDG-TV.

104. The 1996 film *Up Close and Personal* stars Michelle Pfeiffer as the small-town weather reporter and Robert Redford as the veteran news anchor.

105. *Phenomenon.*

106. Mullen's company is known as Endeavor Airlines.

107. Actor Nick Nolte's son Brawley played the role of Sean Mullen.

108. In 1947, MGM released the motion picture *The Bishop's Wife* starring Cary Grant. It provided the inspiration for the 1996 Touchstone film *The Preacher's Wife.*

109. Actor Denzel Washington plays the character Dudley, an angel sent to Earth to provide a little heavenly intervention.

110. *Con Air* (1997).

111. *Con Air* received the nomination for the song "How Do I Live."

112. *The Horse Whisperer.*

113. *Six Days, Seven Nights.*

114. *The Waterboy.*

115. *Beloved*, starring Oprah Winfrey and Danny Glover.

116. *Enemy of the State*. The film stars Will Smith as attorney Dean. With the help of ex-intelligence operative Brill, played by actor Gene Hackman, Dean regains his former life.

117. *Rushmore*. In the film an unlikely friendship and rivalry develops between Fischer and the school's chief benefactor, the billionaire Mr. Blume, played by actor Bill Murray. Rushmore is the name of the academy that Fischer attends.

118. *Armageddon* (1998) became the top-grossing film of any studio. *Armageddon* also edged out *Pretty Woman* (1990), which was at that point the company's highest earning live-action release. In 1999, *The Sixth Sense* took over the crown as top-grossing live-action film.

119. *A Civil Action*.

120. *10 Things I Hate About You*. In the film strict household rules forbid Bianca from dating until her sister Kat gets a boyfriend. Bianca, desperate for romance, turns to a scheme to match Kat with her equivalent, a guy with an infamous reputation.

121. *Instinct*. A book by Daniel Quinn entitled *Ishmael* provided the basis for the film.

122. *Eaters of the Dead* is the basis for the Touchstone Pictures film *The 13th Warrior*. The film stars actor Antonio Banderas, who is an ambassador recruited by a band of warriors. Banderas's character is then forced to join their battle against mysterious creatures known for consuming every living thing in their path.

123. Robin Williams stars as the two-hundred-year-old android Andrew Martin in *Bicentennial Man*.

124. Composer James Horner provided the music for *Bicentennial Man*. Horner also scored such films as *Apollo 13*, *Field of Dreams*, *Braveheart*, *Ransom*, and *Mighty Joe Young*.

125. The film is known as *Mission to Mars*, the same name used for a former attraction at Disneyland and Walt Disney World. The film tells the story of a rescue mission in outer space after a scheduled mission to Mars meets disaster.

126. A sphinx serves as the logo for Hollywood Pictures.

127. Actor John Goodman plays exterminator Delbert McClintock in *Arachnophobia*.

128. *Run*.

129. Actors Jerry Orbach and James Woods who starred in the film *Straight Talk* respectively provided the voices of the character Lumiere in *Beauty and The Beast* (1991) and Hades in *Hercules* (1997).

130. *A Stranger Among Us* (1992).

131. Eddie Murphy plays con man Thomas Jefferson Johnson in the film *The Distinguished Gentleman*.

132. Thomas Jefferson Johnson is a con man who runs for Congress.

133. Actor Noah Wyle, Dr. John Truman Carter III in the television series *ER*, played a Nazi in *Swing Kids*.

134. Ming-Na Wen provided the speaking voice of Mulan in the 1998 full-length animated feature by that same name.

135. The role of Hooker was played by legendary actor Charlton Heston. It is Hooker who agrees to take care of Doc Holliday.

136. *Quiz Show* (1994).

137. John Williams. The film also received an Academy Award nomination that year for Best Original Dramatic Score. Williams may best be remembered for providing the music for such motion pictures as the *Star Wars* series and the *Indiana Jones* films.

138. *Too Much.*

139. *White Squall*, and it stars Jeff Bridges.

140. *Celtic Pride* (1996), starring actor Damon Wayans as the opposing team's star athlete.

141. Legendary film director Francis Ford Coppola.

142. The 1996 Academy Award for Best Song was received by the film *Evita* for the song "You Must Love Me," sung by Madonna with music by Andrew Lloyd Webber and lyrics by Tim Rice.

143. Actor Antonio Banderas portrays the narrator, Ché Guevara.

144. The city of Budapest, Hungary, was used for the filming of the funeral procession of Eva Perón in *Evita* (1996). Filmmakers decided not to use Buenos Aires because the city looked too modern.

145. Actor Jonathan Pryce plays Argentine dictator Juan Perón. Pryce also played the part of Mr. Dark in the 1983 Disney film *Something Wicked This Way Comes*.

146. The film *Grosse Pointe Blank* (1997) tells the story of Martin, a professional assassin played by John Cusack, who returns home to attend his ten-year high school reunion.

147.   *G.I. Jane* (1997) was originally known by that working title. In the film, actress Demi Moore portrays an ambitious Navy Intelligence officer who is chosen as the first female candidate for the Navy's exclusive SEAL squad.

148.   Jim Carrey. Carrey provides the narration and appears at the conclusion of the film as a grown-up Joe.

149.   *The Sixth Sense* (1999). The part of Cole Sear is played by Haley Joel Osment. Osment earlier provided the voice of Chip in the made-for-video film *Beauty and the Beast: The Enchanted Christmas* (1997).

150.   *Mystery, Alaska* (1999). The title refers to the small Alaskan town the amateur hockey team is from.

Selected Disney Films

Mary Poppins

August 29, 1964

Questions:

1. According to George Banks, how many nannies have worked for the family prior to Mary Poppins—one, three, six, or ten?

2. What does Mary Poppins call the first game that she and the children play in the nursery?

3. What traditional English-style hunt do Mary Poppins, Bert, and the two children find themselves involved in during their Jolly Holiday?

4. According to the song "Chim Chim Cher-ee," what profession is described as being on the "bottom-most rung?"

5. What does Michael Banks do that causes a run on the bank?

6. What song does Mr. George Banks sing after he discovers that he has been fired from his position at the bank?

7. Who is the first to remark that the wind has changed to the west?

8. Who is the last person to say something to Mary Poppins?

9. What popular British character actor plays the constable?

10. What legendary actor and later Disney board member presented the Academy Award for Best Actress to Julie Andrews for her portrayal in *Mary Poppins* (1964)?

Mary Poppins

Answers:

1. The Banks family has gone through six nannies before employing Mary Poppins.

2. Mary Poppins calls the game "Well begun is half done." In other words, "Let's tidy up the nursery."

3. They find themselves in the midst of a fox hunt.

4. Chimney sweep.

5. George Banks takes the children to the bank and he and Mr. Dawes, Sr., attempt to get Michael to open up an account. Mr. Dawes, Sr., snatches the tuppence out of Michael's hands. Michael then shouts and grabs the money back. The other account holders start a mad run on the bank, thinking the bank is refusing to return money from accounts.

6. George Banks sings "A Man Has Dreams," set to same tune as "The Life I Lead."

7. Admiral Boom is the first to remark about the change in the wind's direction. The wind change also indicates that Mary Poppins will be leaving because she came in on an east wind.

8. As Mary Poppins begins to fly away, Bert says, "Good-bye, Mary Poppins, don't stay away too long."

9. British character actor Arthur Treacher plays the constable. Treacher may best be remembered for a popular chain of fish-and-chips restaurants that bear his name.

10. Sidney Poitier presented the Academy Award for Best Actress to Julie Andrews.

Splash

March 9, 1984

Questions:

1. Where did the mermaid and Allen Bauer first meet?

2. At what famous landmark does the mermaid first make her appearance on land?

3. How many days does the mermaid have to stay in human form?

4. What catchy Disney song does Allen Bauer sing to himself in the film?

5. What gift does Allen give to the mermaid and what gift does she in turn give to him?

Splash

Answers:

1. They first met when Allen was eight years old and on vacation with his family in Cape Cod, Massachusetts. Allen accidentally fell overboard while the family was taking a scenic cruise of the area. The mermaid rescues Allen by breathing air into his lungs.
2. The mermaid first makes her appearance at the Statue of Liberty.
3. The mermaid has six days until the moon is full to remain in her human form.
4. Allen sings to himself "Zip-a-Dee-Doo-Dah" from the 1946 motion picture *Song of the South*.
5. Allen gives her a small music box and she gives him the large fountain featuring a mermaid, which the two saw in the park.

Pretty Woman

March 23, 1990

Questions:

1. What popular actor plays the part of Edward Lewis and what does he do for a living?

2. What is the name of the hotel manager of the Regent Beverly Wilshire who helps Vivian?

3. What is Edward's phobia?

4. On what famous California street is Vivian treated rudely and asked not to shop there again?

5. Instead of buying out James Morse, what does Edward offer him?

Pretty Woman

Answers:

1. Actor Richard Gere plays Edward Lewis, a financier who buys out financially depressed companies and then sells them in their entirety or in pieces. His company's name is Lewis Enterprises, Inc.
2. The hotel manager is Bernard Thompson, but Vivian prefers to call him "Barney" for short.
3. Edward is afraid of heights.
4. Vivian is told by the boutique owners on Rodeo Drive in Beverly Hills not to shop there again.
5. Instead of buying out Morse's company, Edward encourages him to be his partner. Edward's change of heart comes from Vivian, who convinces him that building things is much more rewarding than just buying out companies.

Father of the Bride

December 20, 1991

Questions:

1. What is the name of the athletic sneaker company owned by George Banks?

2. The story concerns the events leading up to George and Nina's daughter Annie's wedding. Where did Annie meet her husband-to-be Bryan MacKenzie?

3. What does Bryan MacKenzie do for a living?

4. What is the full name of the couple's wedding coordinator and his assistant?

5. What was the one thing George Banks wanted to do with his daughter at the wedding reception which he never did?

Father of the Bride

Answers:

1. SideKicks.
2. The two met while Annie was studying abroad in Italy.
3. Bryan classifies himself as an Independent Communications Consultant. Or as Annie says, "He's a computer genius!"
4. The wedding coordinator is Franck Eggelhoffer played by actor Martin Short, and his assistant is Howard Weinstein, from the Weinsteins of Hong Kong. The part of Howard is played by actor B. D. Wong.
5. What George wanted most of all was to dance with his daughter at the wedding reception. Unfortunately, everything that could have gone wrong did for George and he never got the opportunity to dance with Annie.

The Muppet Christmas Carol

December 11, 1992

Questions:

1. What character serves as the narrator for the film?

2. What actor plays the part of Ebenezer Scrooge?

3. What two characters play the parts of Ebenezer Scrooge's former partners, Robert and Jacob Marley?

4. Who plays Ebenezer Scrooge's trusted and faithful bookkeeper, Bob Cratchit?

5. What kind of animals make up the rest of Ebenezer Scrooge's bookkeeping staff?

6. Who plays the part of Bob Cratchit's loving wife, Emily?

7. How many children do Bob and Emily Cratchit have?

8. Which two characters are collecting for the poor, and are originally rejected by Ebenezer Scrooge?

9. In one of the scenes, Ebenezer Scrooge is shown images of his past. What characters play the part of his former school master and his first employer?

10. Who is recruited by Ebenezer Scrooge, as the film concludes, to go to the market and purchase the prize turkey in the shop's window?

The Muppet Christmas Carol

Answers:

1. Gonzo serves as the film's narrator playing the part of author Charles Dickens. Gonzo is accompanied by his sidekick, Rizzo the Rat.
2. Michael Caine.
3. The ghostly images of Robert and Jacob, who warn Ebenezer of his wrongdoings, are played by Muppets Waldorf and Statler.
4. Kermit the Frog.
5. A bunch of rats.
6. Emily Cratchit is played by Miss Piggy, and even though they are poor she still manages to wear her jewelry.
7. Bob and Emily Cratchit have four children; two frogs, including Tiny Tim, and two pigs.
8. Dr. Bunsen Honeydew and his trusted assistant Beaker are collecting for the poor.
9. Sam the Eagle is Ebenezer Scrooge's former schoolmaster and Fozzie Bear plays his former employer, Fozziwig, who owns a rubber chicken company.
10. Bean Bunny.

Tim Burton's The Nightmare Before Christmas

October 22, 1993

Questions:

1. What actor provides the narration for the opening of the film?

2. What is the name of Jack Skellington's girlfriend?

3. What is the name of the evil scientist and who does he have a mad crush on?

4. Who is considered the meanest demon in all of Halloweentown?

5. What is so unusual about the mayor of Halloweentown?

6. What does Sally place in Dr. Finkelstein's soup causing him to fall unconscious and giving her the opportunity to escape?

7. What object serves as Jack Skellington's Santa Claus sleigh?

8. How many reindeer are used to pull Jack's Santa Claus sleigh and what was so unusual about them?

9. During what song does Jack Skellington discover the joy of the Christmas holiday?

10. Who wrote the musical score for the film *Tim Burton's The Nightmare Before Christmas*?

Tim Burton's The Nightmare Before Christmas

Answers:

1. Actor Patrick Stewart provides the narration for the opening of the film. Stewart is perhaps best remembered for his portrayal of Captain Jean-Luc Picard in the television series *Star Trek: The Next Generation*.
2. Jack's girlfriend is Sally, voiced by actress Catherine O'Hara.
3. The evil scientist is Dr. Finkelstein and he has a mad crush on Sally.
4. The nasty Oogie Boogie.
5. The mayor has two faces, one that shows a smile and the other, a look of fright.
6. The mixture is known as "Deadly Nightshade."
7. Jack's sleigh is made from a coffin.
8. Jack has the skeletal remains of three reindeer pulling his sleigh.
9. "What's This."
10. Songwriter Danny Elfman wrote the film's musical score. Elfman also provided the singing voice for the character Jack Skellington.

The Santa Clause

November 11, 1994

Questions:

1. After unintentionally destroying their planned meal, where does Scott take his son, Charlie, for dinner on Christmas Eve?

2. Who does Scott Calvin discover on his roof that one particular Christmas Eve?

3. What does Scott Calvin do for a living?

4. What story does Scott Calvin read to his son, Charlie, prompting him to think the whole experience was just a dream?

5. Scott Calvin can't understand his sudden weight gain and his aging hair, so he decides to go to his doctor to see if there is any explanation he can give. When the doctor checks the condition of his heart, what song does he hear through his stethoscope?

6. What is the name of the elf who is in charge of the North Pole's Research and Development Department?

7. According to Elf Judy, what has taken her 1,200 years to perfect?

8. What does Scott Calvin place around his waist as a reference to Tim Allen's television series *Home Improvement*?

9. What does FedEx deliver to Scott Calvin one day?

10. What does Santa Claus give to Charlie, Laura, and Neil near the conclusion of the film?

The Santa Clause

Answers:

1. Denny's, because they are always open. Unfortunately, the restaurant is out of many of the traditional holiday favorites, including eggnog.
2. Santa Claus.
3. Scott designs and markets toys.
4. "'Twas the Night Before Christmas."
5. Instead of the typical beat of a heart the doctor hears the song "Jingle Bells."
6. The elf's name is Quintin. The name is actually a clever reference to the classic character "Q," who has a similar role in all of the James Bond films.
7. According to Elf Judy, it has taken 1,200 years to perfect her hot cocoa making. She says her secret in making her hot cocoa is "not too hot, extra chocolate, shaken, not stirred." The expression is yet another reference to the James Bond films, for Bond says "Shaken, not stirred" whenever he asks for a martini.
8. Scott Calvin, played by actor Tim Allen, in one of the scenes places a tool belt around his waist, a direct reference to Allen's television series, *Home Improvement*.
9. FedEx delivers to Scott boxes and boxes of Santa's "Good and Bad List."
10. Scott's son, Charlie, gets a soccer ball, his ex-wife gets the board game she always wanted, the "Mystery Date Game," and Neil gets his Oscar Mayer Wiener Whistle, a gift he, too, has wanted since he was young.

Toy Story

November 22, 1995

Questions:

1. In early planning for the film, what character was going to be called Lunar Larry?

2. What present does Andy receive for his birthday which causes his favorite toy, Woody, to become jealous?

3. What is the name of Andy's little sister?

4. What is the name of the evil emperor from whom Buzz Lightyear and the Space Rangers defend the galaxy?

5. What is the name of the nasty boy who lives next door to Andy?

6. What toys are sent on a reconnaissance mission to find out what Andy is getting for his birthday?

7. What actor provides the voice of the pig, Hamm?

8. What is the name of the interactive restaurant arcade to which Woody and Buzz Lightyear hitch a ride in order to reunite with their master, Andy?

9. Throughout the course of the film, what toy does Mr. Potato Head keep wishing that either Andy or Molly would receive as a present?

10. What popular 1960s television series' theme song is played when Buzz Lightyear and Woody find themselves in Sid's bedroom?

Toy Story

Answers:

1. Lunar Larry was the early name for Buzz Lightyear.
2. Andy receives a Buzz Lightyear Space Ranger action figure for his birthday. Woody perceives this as a threat and fears he will be replaced as Andy's favorite toy.
3. Andy's little sister is Molly.
4. Emperor Zurg.
5. The nasty boy next door to Andy is Sid. One of his nastiest traits is his love of tormenting and destroying toys.
6. The Green Army Men.
7. Actor John Ratzenberger provided the voice of the wisecracking Hamm. Ratzenberger may best be remembered for the character Cliff Clavin on the long-running television series *Cheers* (1982–1993).
8. Pizza Planet.
9. Mr. Potato Head appropriately wishes for a Mrs. Potato Head doll. At last, as the film ends, Mr. Potato Head gets his wish.
10. Appropriately, the theme from *The Munsters* (1964–1966) plays when Buzz and Woody meet the mutant toys in Sid's room.

James and the Giant Peach

April 12, 1996

Questions:

1. To what city does James long to travel?

2. How many bugs join James on his incredible journey?

3. What insect serves as a father figure to James, providing him support and encouragement?

4. What Academy Award–winning actress provides the voice of the cool and resourceful Miss Spider?

5. What type of birds does James use to enable the peach to fly?

James and the Giant Peach

Answers:

1. James wishes to go to New York City more than anywhere. It was James's father who used to tell him that New York City is where "dreams come true."
2. Six bugs join James—Centipede, Earthworm, Ladybug, Glowworm, Grasshopper, and Spider.
3. Grasshopper.
4. Actress Susan Sarandon provides the voice of Miss Spider.
5. James uses a flock of seagulls to lift the peach and carry it through the sky.

101 Dalmatians

November 27, 1996

Questions:

1. What is unique about the gloves worn by Cruella De Vil in the film?

2. Cruella's personalized license plate spells out what?

3. What kind of business does Cruella De Vil run?

4. What does Roger Radcliff do for a living in the film?

5. What song from the 1970 full-length animated feature *The Aristocats* can also be heard in *101 Dalmatians*?

101 Dalmatians

Answers

1. Cruella's gloves have fingernails on them. They could best be described as claws.
2. Cruella's personalized license plate reads "DEV IL."
3. Cruella is the head of her own fashion company known as the House of De Vil.
4. Roger writes computer games in the 1996 film, *101 Dalmatians*. In the 1961 animated feature, Roger is a songwriter.
5. "Ev'rybody Wants to Be a Cat."

The Ultimate Disney Trivia Book 4
128

George of the Jungle

July 16, 1997

Questions:

1. What popular musical group performed the film's title song?

2. What popular actor portrays the part of the lovable but inept King of the Jungle, George?

3. According to the story, what event occurred which caused George to be raised in the jungle?

4. Where in Africa did George grow up?

5. How does George first meet the beautiful adventure-seeking heiress, Ursula Stanhope?

6. What is the name of George's trusted doggie?

7. Where does Ursula take George after he is accidentally injured by Lyle?

8. To what famous department store does Ursula take George in order to outfit him in more appropriate clothing for his new urban environment?

9. How does George deliver himself back to his home in Africa?

10. A parody of which Disney feature film is found at the end of the film?

George of the Jungle

Answers:

1. The title song "George of the Jungle" was performed by the musical group The Presidents of the United States of America.
2. Actor Brendan Fraser plays the part of George.
3. There was a plane crash when George was an infant and he was unfortunately separated from the rest of his group and forced to grow up in the jungle.
4. The mythical place, located in the heart of Africa, is known as Bukuva.
5. George saves Ursula from a lion when she and her fiancé, Lyle Van de Groot, go wandering into the jungle on their own.
6. George's doggie is actually an elephant named Shep. Yet Shep has all of the mannerisms of a dog and George even affectionately refers to him as his "big gray peanut-loving poochie."
7. Ursula flies George to San Francisco so he can receive medical treatment for his injuries.
8. Ursula takes George to Neiman-Marcus.
9. George places himself in a crate and has United Parcel Service (UPS) send him home.
10. After George and Ursula's marriage and the birth of their son, George, Jr., a parody of the "Circle of Life" sequence from *The Lion King* (1994) occurs at the end of the film.

Armageddon

....

July 1, 1998

Questions:

1. What facility hosted the film's world premiere?

2. What famous actor provides the narration as the film opens?

3. What type of business does Harry Stamper own and why does the government need his assistance?

4. What are the names of the two space shuttles that set out on the mission to destroy the giant meteor?

5. What name is given to the giant meteor?

6. The story is about an approaching giant meteor the size of Texas which is on a direct course to Earth. When it does hit, it will obliterate all life on Earth as we know it. How many days does the team at NASA have in order to come up with a plan of action?

7. The government agrees to let Harry bring his own team into space for the rescue mission. What is the final request they make once they agree to join Harry and change the course of the meteor?

8. What does the mission patch worn by the shuttle rescue team say?

9. What 1960s song do some of Harry's team sing as they wait to board the shuttles?

10. What does Harry hand to A. J. that he wants given to Dan Truman, the executive director of NASA who orchestrated the mission?

Armageddon

Answers:

1. On June 29, 1998, the Kennedy Space Center in Florida hosted the world premiere of the film.
2. Charlton Heston.
3. Harry owns an offshore oil business known as Stamper Oil. He is known as the world's best driller. NASA believes the only way to deflect the asteroid from hitting Earth is to send up a team, drill 800 feet into the object, and detonate a nuclear bomb. Actor Bruce Willis plays the role of Harry Stamper.
4. The two shuttles are the Freedom and the Independence. They both are the next generation of shuttles developed by NASA known as X-71.
5. A retired military officer by the name of Karl first spots the giant meteor through his telescope and because he is the first to observe the object, he is given the opportunity to name it. Karl gave it the name "Dottie" after his wife, not meaning it as a compliment.
6. They have eighteen days.
7. The team makes several requests, such as the dismissal of parking tickets, but their final request is never to pay taxes again.
8. "Freedom—Independence for All Mankind."
9. Some of the team sing the 1960s song "Leaving on a Jet Plane" prior to boarding the shuttles.
10. Harry rips the mission patch from his suit and hands it to A. J. and instructs him to give it to Dan Truman. Truman has confided in Harry at one point that he has always wanted to travel on his own shuttle mission, but that his disability has made this impossible. Actor Ben Affleck plays the part of A. J. and Billy Bob Thornton plays Truman.

The Parent Trap

July 29, 1998

Questions:

1. What nickname do both Hallie and Annie use to describe their father's fiancée, Meredith Blake?

2. What is the name of the camp at which the two girls meet by chance?

3. What are the full names of Hallie and Annie?

4. Where do Hallie and Annie live?

5. Where did the two girls' mother and father first meet?

6. What types of business do their father and mother own?

7. How old are Hallie and Annie?

8. Which actress from the original 1961 version of the film is also featured in the updated 1998 release of *The Parent Trap*?

9. How do the girls attempt to re-create their parents' first date?

10. Which song from the original 1961 version of *The Parent Trap* does one of the twins sing?

The Parent Trap

Answers:

1. The two girls refer to their father's fiancée as Cruella, a reference to the character in the film *One Hundred and One Dalmatians*.
2. Camp Walden.
3. The two girls are Hallie Parker and Annie James.
4. Hallie lives with her father, Nick Parker, in Napa, California, and Annie lives with her mother, Elizabeth James, in London, England.
5. Nick and Elizabeth first met in 1986 on a sailing of the *Queen Elizabeth 2* across the Atlantic. It was a picture that Nick and Elizabeth had taken on the ship that helped Hallie and Annie realize they were sisters.
6. Nick is the owner of Parker Knoll Vineyards in Napa Valley, California. Elizabeth is a fashion designer who specializes in wedding gowns. Her boutique is appropriately named Elizabeth James.
7. According to the two girls, they will be twelve on October 11.
8. Actress Joanna Barnes appears in both versions of *The Parent Trap*. Barnes plays the part of Margaret Blake's mother, Vicki. She played the daughter, then known also as Vicki, in the original film.
9. By using their allowance money and a little help from their grandfather, the two rent a yacht and decorate it with references to the *Queen Elizabeth 2*. They also arrange an intimate dinner for two onboard.
10. "Let's Get Together."

A Bug's Life

November 25, 1998

Questions:

1. What is the name of the misfit ant that takes it upon himself to travel to the city in order to recruit a bunch of bigger bugs to help his colony defend itself from a swarm of greedy grasshoppers?

2. What is the name of the ant who is training to be queen of the colony?

3. What is the name of the queen's pet?

4. What is the name of the obnoxious owner of the run-down flea circus?

5. What is the name of the male ladybug who cannot understand why everyone just assumes he is a girl?

6. What is the name of the lovable little caterpillar who dreams of being a beautiful butterfly?

7. What is the name of the cute little ant who continues to believe in Flik?

8. What is the name of the greedy and vicious leader of the grasshoppers that bullies the ant colony into harvesting their food supply?

9. What does the ant colony construct in an effort to scare away Hopper and his gang?

10. What type of bug is Molt, and what happens to him at the conclusion of the film?

A Bug's Life

Answers:

1. The misfit ant is Flik and his voice is provided by actor Dave Foley.
2. The queen-in-training is Princess Atta, voiced by actress Julia Louis-Dreyfus. Louis-Dreyfus may be best remembered for playing the part of Elaine on the comedy series *Seinfeld* (1990–1998).
3. Aphie.
4. The owner of the flea circus is P. T. Flea, voiced by actor John Ratzenberger.
5. The male ladybug is Francis, voiced by actor Denis Leary.
6. Heimlich.
7. Dot.
8. The leader of the grasshoppers is Hopper, voiced by actor Kevin Spacey.
9. A mechanical bird.
10. Molt is the bumbling brother of Hopper, who eventually joins the flea circus at the conclusion of the film. The voice of Molt is provided by actor Richard Kind.

Mighty Joe Young

December 25, 1998

Questions:

1. Which motion picture provided the inspiration for the Disney film?

2. What is the name of the mountain region located in Central Africa where the fifteen-foot gorilla Joe lives?

3. What is the name of the woman who is friend to Joe?

4. What is the name of the zoologist who, while on an exploration, discovers the mighty gorilla?

5. Joe jumps through what letter of the famous Hollywood sign in an effort to run from the authorities?

Mighty Joe Young

Answers:

1. *Mighty Joe Young* is a remake of the original movie by that same title released by Argosy/RKO in 1949. The original film won an Academy Award for Best Special Effects.

2. Joe lives near a remote African village in the Pangani Mountains. Many believe the fifteen-foot gorilla is the sacred guardian and defender of the village.

3. Joe's only friend is Jill Young. Both of their mothers were killed by poachers twenty years before.

4. The zoologist's name is Gregg O'Hara, played by actor Bill Paxton. In the original film actor Ben Johnson played the similar role of Gregg Ford.

5. Joe jumps through an *O* in the Hollywood sign.

Walt Disney Theatrical Productions

Questions:

1. Which two actors who appeared in the theatrical production *King David* provided voices in two previous full-length animated features?

2. In which city did the theatrical production of *Disney's The Lion King* have its pre-Broadway run?

3. In which New York theater did *Disney's The Lion King* have its Broadway debut?

4. Featured at the New Amsterdam Theater are twelve theater boxes off the stage area. The theater boxes are named after what?

5. What is the Rooftop Theater?

6. How many songs are used in the Broadway production of *Disney's The Lion King*?

7. Which male character from the 1994 full-length animated feature *The Lion King* is played by a woman in the stage version?

8. Which actor originated the role of Mufasa in the Broadway production of *Disney's The Lion King*?

9. How many Tony Awards did *Disney's The Lion King* receive in 1998?

10. The first international production of *Disney's The Lion King* premiered in which country?

11. What story does Belle read to the Beast in the Broadway version of *Disney's Beauty and the Beast*?

12. What actress and actor originated the roles of Belle and the Beast when *Disney's Beauty and the Beast* was introduced to the stage?

13. What Grammy Award-winning Pop and R & B singing artist joined the cast of *Disney's Beauty and the Beast* as Belle in 1998?

14. What actress who originated the role of Annie in the Broadway production by that same name joined the cast of *Disney's Beauty and the Beast* as Belle in 1999?

15. What was the first fully staged Walt Disney Theatrical Production developed as a musical from material not drawn from an existing animated feature?

16. Who are the composers of the theatrical production *Aida*?

17. The theatrical production *Aida* is based on an opera by whom?

18. When did *Disney's Beauty and the Beast* move from its Broadway home at the Palace Theater to the Lunt-Fontanne Theater?

19. What was the first Disney musical to premiere in a foreign language?

20. The song "There's Been a Change in Me" is featured in which Disney theatrical production?

Walt Disney
Theatrical Productions

....

Answers:

1. Actress Judy Kuhn, who played the part of Saul's daughter, Michal, provided the singing voice of Pocahontas, and actor Roger Bart, who was Saul's son, Jonathan, was the singing voice of the teen Hercules.

2. On July 8, 1997, the theatrical production of *Disney's The Lion King* made its initial run at the Orpheum Theater in Minneapolis, Minnesota.

3. *The Lion King* had its premiere on Broadway on October 10, 1997, at the New Amsterdam Theater, located on 42nd Street west of Broadway, in New York City.

4. Each of the twelve theater boxes is named after a different flower, such as violet, rose, buttercup, peony, heliothrope, and water lily.

5. The Rooftop Theater is a former 350-seat facility that is located above the New Amsterdam Theater. In the early days of the New Amsterdam the Rooftop Theater played host to a collection of after-hours Vaudeville-type shows.

6. A total of thirteen songs are used during the production. Five of the songs appeared in the 1994 animated version of *The Lion King*.

7. The character Rafiki in the Broadway version of *The Lion King* is now performed by a woman. South African singer Tsidii Le Loka originated the role.

8. Actor Samuel E. Wright originated the role of the mighty Mufasa in the Broadway version of the story. Wright may best be remembered by Disney fans for providing the voice of the crab Sebastian in the 1989 full-length animated feature *The Little Mermaid*.

9. Six: Best Scenic Design, Best Lighting Design, Best Costume Design, Best Choreography, Best Director of a Musical, and Best Musical. Julie Taymor made Broadway history when she became the first woman to win the Tony Award for Best Director of a Musical.

10. On December 20, 1998, *Disney's The Lion King* opened at the Haru Theatre in Tokyo, Japan.

11. Belle reads the story of "King Arthur" to the Beast.

12. Actress Susan Egan originated the role of Belle and actor Terrence Mann that of the Beast. Egan provided the voice of Megara in the 1997 full-length animated feature *Hercules*. Mann, a Broadway veteran of many roles, including Jean Valjean in *Les Miserables*, also had a recurring role on the animated television series *Gargoyles*.

13. Grammy Award–winning pop and R & B singing artist Toni Braxton joined the cast as Belle in 1998.

14. Actress Andrea McArdle, best known for her role as the red-haired orphan girl in the Broadway production of *Annie*, joined the cast of *Disney's Beauty and the Beast* as Belle in 1999.

15. *Aida*. During the production's initial run, the title of the musical was *Elaborate Lives: The Legend of Aida*.

16. Elton John and Tim Rice. Rice and John worked previously together on the 1994 full-length animated feature *The Lion King*.

17. The tragic opera about an enslaved Nubian princess is based on a work by Giuseppe Verdi.

18. *Disney's Beauty and the Beast* held its last performance at the Palace Theater on September 5, 1999, and opened two months later at the Lunt-Fontanne Theater on November 12, 1999. *Beauty and the Beast* became the longest-running production in the history of the Palace Theater.

19. *Der Glockner von Notre Dame*, a German version of *The Hunchback of Notre Dame*, opened on June 5, 1999, at the 1,800-seat Musical Theatre on Marlene Dietrich Platz in Berlin, Germany. Academy Award–winning songwriters Alan Menken and Stephen Schwartz headed the creative effort. The show was performed entirely in German without subtitles, making it the first American musical to premiere in a foreign language.

20. The song "There's Been a Change in Me" was added to *Disney's Beauty and the Beast* in 1999. The song is performed by Belle after returning from the Beast's castle so that she may save her father. Remarkably, the song was added five years after the show made its debut on Broadway.

Disney Cruise Line

....

Questions:

1. Which ship is longer: the *Disney Magic*, the *Disney Wonder*, or *Titanic*?

2. The ship's registry for the *Disney Magic* and *Disney Wonder* is in which country?

3. Who christened the *Disney Magic* and the *Disney Wonder*?

4. An image of Mickey in which of his roles appears on the front of the *Disney Magic* and in which on the *Disney Wonder*?

5. What color are the lifeboats on the Disney Cruise Line ships?

6. Which animated characters are suspended from the back of the *Disney Magic* and *Disney Wonder* ships?

7. The beginning notes of what popular Disney song can be heard from the horn of the *Disney Magic* and *Disney Wonder*?

8. How many funnel stacks do each of the ships have?

9. Statues of which characters are featured in the ship's atrium lobby of the *Disney Magic* and the *Disney Wonder*?

10. What part of Mickey's body holds up the slide at the children's pool?

11. What is the name of the nighttime entertainment areas located on the *Disney Magic* and on the *Disney Wonder*?

12. What is the name of the "teen only" coffeehouse?

13. What is the name of the 1,040-seat theater located on the *Disney Magic* and *Disney Wonder*, which plays host to a collection of Broadway-style shows?

14. What is the name of the restaurant located on the *Disney Magic* and the *Disney Wonder* that changes colors as each new course appears?

15. Which characters from *The Little Mermaid* and *Beauty and the Beast* provide the inspiration for restaurants onboard the *Disney Magic* and *Disney Wonder*?

16. What is the name of the adult beach located on Castaway Cay?

17. What do the letters that appear on the former landing strip on Castaway Cay spell out?

18. What country runs the Castaway Cay post office?

19. What famous whale provides the name for the children's archaeological dig site where one can find the apparent remains of an ancient whale ?

20. Who is considered the Master Chef on Castaway Cay?

21. What is the name of the island's main shop which features exclusive Castaway Cay logo merchandise?

22. True or false: passengers board a launch to land on Castaway Cay.

23. Which character's hands are featured on the clock tower as you enter the Port Canaveral Terminal building?

24. What images are detailed in the 13,000-square-foot tile floor on the second story of the Port Canaveral Terminal?

25. What is the name of the toll road that runs between the Walt Disney World Resort and the Port Canaveral Terminal?

Disney Cruise Line

Answers:

1. The *Disney Magic* and *Disney Wonder* are the same length, and both are longer and wider than *Titanic*, each being 964 feet long and 106 feet wide. *Titanic* was 882¼ feet long and 93 feet wide. If the *Disney Magic* or *Disney Wonder* were any longer or wider, then passage through the Panama Canal would not be possible. Remarkably, the two Disney ships are nearly as long as the Eiffel Tower is high.

2. Both ships' registry is the Bahamas. Due to tax considerations, most cruise line companies use either the Bahamas or Liberia for their ships' registry.

3. On July 28, 1998, Roy E. Disney's wife, Patricia, officially christened the *Disney Magic*. The *Disney Wonder* was christened on October 1, 1999, by Tinker Bell.

4. An image of Mickey featured as the Sorcerer's Apprentice appears on the *Disney Magic*, and as Steamboat Willie on the *Disney Wonder*.

5. The lifeboats are yellow. The Disney Cruise Line was actually granted special permission to use the color so it would match one of the colors associated with Mickey Mouse. Traditionally, maritime law requires that such boats need to be painted orange.

6. Goofy is suspended from the back of the *Disney Magic,* but on the *Disney Wonder* you can see Huey causing mischief at Uncle Donald's expense while two other sets of eyes look on.

7. The horn plays the first notes of "When You Wish Upon a Star" from *Pinocchio.*

8. Both ships have two funnel stacks which help create the look of a classic luxury liner. One funnel stack is functional, while the second houses the ESPN Skybox, a sports bar.

9. A statue of Mickey dressed as a helmsman is situated in the atrium lobby of the *Disney Magic* and Ariel from *The Little Mermaid* is featured on the *Disney Wonder.*

10. Mickey's hand is carefully positioned to hold up the children's slide, enabling young guests the opportunity to splash down into a pool that is shaped like Mickey's head.

11. The entertainment district is called Beat Street on the *Disney Magic.* On the *Disney Wonder*, the same area, featuring a collection of lounges and clubs, is called Route 66.

12. The "teen only" coffeehouse is called as Common Grounds.

13. The theater is called the Walt Disney Theatre. Both ships also feature a 270-seat Buena Vista Theatre, where movies are shown and lectures are held by guest lecturers.

14. The restaurant is known as Animator's Palate, and as the evening progresses, the walls, paintings, and other props change from black-and-white to color.

15. The characters Lumiere and King Triton each have elegant restaurants named after them onboard the *Disney Magic* and *Disney Wonder,* respectively.

16. The adult beach located on the private island of Castaway Cay is known as Serenity Bay Beach.

17. From the air, the letters spell out "Castaway Cay."

18. The Castaway Cay Post Office is run by the government of The Bahamas.

19. According to the story line, the apparent remains of an ancient whale can be found at Monstro Point.

20. The Master Chef's name is Cookie and he serves up his specialties at Cookie's Bar-B-Q.

21. The shop is known as "She Sells SeaShells and everything else!"

22. False. The ocean bottom was dredged to provide a docking area where the ships can tie up.

23. A whimsical clock featuring Mickey Mouse's hands is above the entrance to the Port Canaveral Terminal building.

24. Florida and the Bahamas are beautifully detailed in the floor's exquisite tile work, along with images of sea life, birds, reptiles, a mermaid, and even Cinderella Castle.

25. Route 528, also known as the Bee Line Expressway.

Disneyland

Questions:

1. When Disneyland opened in 1955, how many train stations were located on the Santa Fe and Disneyland Railroad?

2. In what year did Tinker Bell make her first flight over Disneyland?

3. Props from which 1961 Disney film were once on display in the Main Street Opera House?

4. Where in Disneyland could guests once view vintage films such as *The Phantom of the Opera,* featuring Lon Chaney, and *The Great Train Robbery*?

5. What is the name of the elegantly appointed caboose that has been used for transporting special guests and VIPs on the Disneyland Railroad?

6. Which popular comedian used to work in the Magic Shop at Disneyland when he was younger?

7. Where can one find a version of the famous Greek masks depicting Mickey Mouse as the faces of comedy and tragedy?

8. What popular actor met his former wife, Cyndi, when she appeared as a character in a Main Street parade?

9. In 1997, the Carnation Ice Cream Parlor and the Blue Ribbon Bakery were transformed into what new Main Street, U.S.A., shops?

10. Which one of the following is *not* a mode of transportation that has operated on Main Street, U.S.A.: electric car, fire truck, fire wagon, surrey, horse-drawn streetcar, horseless carriage, omnibus?

11. What is the inscription in the front courtyard of Sleeping Beauty Castle?

12. Which was the first Fantasyland attraction to open after its initial grand opening on July 17, 1955?

13. Which Fantasyland train featured cars named Alice, Bambi, Cinderella, Pinocchio, and Tinkerbelle?

14. What at Disneyland was formerly known as Snow Hill?

15. Which Fantasyland attraction featured the "upside down" room?

16. Which character from the film *Dumbo* (1941) can be heard on the Casey Jr. Circus Train?

17. What are the words to Mr. Toad's creed as featured at the entrance to Mr. Toad's Wild Ride?

18. Whose voice can be heard at the Snow White Grotto?

19. The sign WELLS EXPEDITION that appears in the Matterhorn is a reference to whom?

20. When the Storybook Land Canal Boats was redesigned in 1994, scenes from which two animated features were added to the attraction?

21. Mickey's Toontown can only be accessed by going through which other themed land?

22. What is the number of the engine company at the fire station located in Mickey's Toontown?

23. What was the first attraction to open in Mickey's Toontown after it was officially dedicated on January 24, 1993?

24. Which Mickey's Toontown attraction features Franz Liszt's Hungarian Rhapsody no. 2?

25. What is the Gag Factory?

26. What were the Phantom Boats?

27. What familiar Tomorrowland icon that stood in front of an attraction was removed in 1966, only to have a smaller model added above a refreshment location in 1998?

28. The 3D film *Honey, I Shrunk the Audience* replaced what previous film when new Tomorrowland opened in 1998?

29. Which Tomorrowland attraction was once completely leveled and replaced with essentially the same attraction?

30. A stage was constructed in 1969 in Tomorrowland so guests could view what historical event?

31. What were the ride vehicles called in the former Tomorrowland attraction, Adventure Thru Inner Space?

32. Why is Space Mountain smaller in Disneyland than at the Walt Disney World Magic Kingdom?

33. Which high-speed attraction replaced the WEDway PeopleMover in 1998?

34. When the new Tomorrowland opened in 1998, what became of the Carousel Theater?

35. When the submarines of the Submarine Voyage were officially decommissioned, a ceremony was conducted by the United States Navy and a banner was presented to commemorate the event. Which Disney character officially received the banner?

36. How many attractions were in Adventureland when Disneyland opened in 1955?

37. Which Adventureland attraction was originally designed to be a dinner-theater show?

38. Which Disneyland attraction was sponsored first by United Airlines and later by Dole Pineapple?

39. Name the three Adventureland attractions not inspired by a Disney live-action or animated feature.

40. The Swiss Family Tree House was transformed into what new attraction for Disneyland guests in 1999?

41. Name the actors who originated the three primary roles in the Golden Horseshoe Revue.

42. What early Disneyland attraction was a type of covered wagon?

43. Which actor who starred on the 1960s television series *Hazel* operated a barbecue restaurant in Frontierland for four years?

44. Which Mouseketeer made a special cameo appearance to help celebrate the occasion of the Golden Horseshoe Revue's 10,000th performance?

45. What becomes of the *Mark Twain* riverboat during the nighttime spectacular, *Fantasmic!*?

46. Famous Hollywood cowboy star Tex Ritter provided a voice for which attraction?

47. The five-story plunge that guests take near the conclusion of Splash Mountain is a representation of what scene in the film *Song of the South* (1946)?

48. The arcade located in Critter Country is named after which character?

49. The train station located in New Orleans Square is a replica of a train depot built for which 1949 Disney feature film?

50. Besides the Haunted Mansion, how many other locations within the park have cemeteries?

Disneyland

Answers:

1. When the park opened in 1955, there were only two stations as part of the Santa Fe and Disneyland Railroad. The two stations were located on Main Street, U.S.A., and in Frontierland.

2. Tinker Bell first flew over Disneyland in 1961. (Her first flight at the Walt Disney World Magic Kingdom came twenty-four years later.)

3. *Babes in Toyland.*

4. For a period of time, the Main Street Cinema used to show such vintage silent film classics.

5. The railroad car on the Disneyland Railroad is known as the *Lilly Belle*. It features a wonderful collection of photographs of the Disney family over the years.

6. Steve Martin.

7. Mickey is featured as comedy and tragedy on the bank building located on Main Street, U.S.A.

8. Kevin Costner. Costner's former wife Cyndi used to play the part of Snow White at Disneyland.

9. The Blue Ribbon Bakery was replaced by the Gibson Girl Ice Cream Parlor. The Blue Ribbon Bakery relocated to the former Carnation Ice Cream Parlor location. The Carnation Ice Cream Parlor changed its name to Carnation Café, moving into its former patio.

10. They have *all* at one point been in service as a mode of transportation on Main Street, U.S.A.

11. The inscription is WHEN YOU WISH UPON A STAR YOUR DREAMS COME TRUE.

12. Two weeks after Disneyland celebrated its official grand opening, the Casey Jr. Circus Train opened on July 31, 1955.

13. Between June 10, 1957, and September 30, 1958, the Viewliner trains operated at Disneyland. The Viewliner consisted of two six-car trains designated the Fantasyland Viewliner and the Tomorrowland Viewliner. The Fantasyland cars were named after characters: Alice, Bambi, Cinderella, Pinocchio, and Tinkerbelle (though Tinker Bell was misspelled), while the Tomorrowland cars were named after planets: Jupiter, Mars, Mercury, Saturn, and Venus.

14. Snow Hill was the name given to the small hill on which sat the support tower for the Skyway, before the Matterhorn was built in its place.

15. According to the poster, Alice in Wonderland featured the "upside down" room.

16. The Ringmaster from *Dumbo* (1941) can be heard on the Casey Jr. Circus Train.

17. The creed, which appears at the attraction's entrance reads, TOADI ACCELERATIO SEMPER ABSURDA, meaning "speeding with Toad is always absurd."

18. Snow White's: in 1983, a special recording was done by Adriana Caselotti for the Snow White Grotto. Caselotti had provided the original voice of Snow White for the 1937 animated feature.

19. The sign WELLS EXPEDITION in the Matterhorn is a reference to former president of The Walt Disney Company Frank G. Wells, who died in a helicopter accident on April 3, 1994. The reference in the Matterhorn is appropriate because Wells is noted for his attempt to scale the highest peaks on each continent, failing only to conquer Mount Everest.

20. Scenes from *The Little Mermaid* (1989) and *Aladdin* (1992) were added to the attraction, and Toad Hall from the 1949 animated feature *The Adventures of Ichabod and Mr. Toad* had to be removed to make space.

21. Guests have to pass through Fantasyland in order to get to Mickey's Toontown.

22. The fire station located in Mickey's Toontown houses the 101st Engine Company. The 101 refers to the Dalmatians featured on the Fire Department building.

23. Roger Rabbit's Car Toon Spin opened January 26, 1994.

24. The piece by Franz Liszt can be heard in Roger Rabbit's Car Toon Spin.

25. The Gag Factory is a merchandise shop located in Mickey's Toontown.

26. The Phantom Boats were finned boats which operated briefly in Tomorrowland in 1956.

27. The Moonliner rocket which used to stand in front of the Rocket to the Moon attraction was placed above the Spirit of Refreshment sponsored by Coca-Cola in 1998. The Moonliner is 75 percent of its original size. It was designed by Disney Imagineer and Legend John Hench and noted scientist Wernher von Braun.

28. *Honey, I Shrunk the Audience* replaced *Captain Eo*.

29. Rocket to the Moon/Flight to the Moon.

30. A special stage featuring a large television monitor was constructed in Tomorrowland so guests could view the Apollo 11 Lunar Moon Landing on July 20, 1969.
31. The ride vehicles were themed to the attraction and were known as Atomobiles.
32. Space Mountain in Disneyland had to be slightly scaled down because there was less land available for it at the California park.
33. In 1998, with the opening of a new Tomorrowland, the WEDway PeopleMover was replaced by the high-speed thrill ride Rocket Rods.
34. The Carousel Theater originally served as the home for the Carousel of Progress and later the multistage production America Sings. In 1998 it became Innoventions.
35. The ceremony began when one of the submarines, the *Nautilus*, made a ceremonial circuit around the lagoon and the banner was presented to Donald Duck, who was wearing his sailor suit.

36. One. The Jungle Cruise was the only Adventureland attraction open on July 17, 1955. The next major attractions to open were the Swiss Family Tree House in 1962 and the Enchanted Tiki Room in 1963.

37. The Enchanted Tiki Room was originally designed to be a restaurant, with Audio-Animatronics® entertainment, but the idea had to be abandoned after it was determined that the facility would have limited seating capacity.

38. The Enchanted Tiki Room. United Airlines was a logical sponsor of the attraction because of the extensive service the carrier provided to the Hawaiian Islands, and, of course, Dole is closely associated with Hawaii.

39. The Indiana Jones Adventure, Enchanted Tiki Room, and the Jungle Cruise boats.

40. The Swiss Family Tree House was transformed into Tarzan's Treehouse in 1999 to coincide with the release of the full-length animated feature.

41. The first stars were Donald Novis, "the silver-toned tenor," Judy Marsh, and comedian Wally Boag. Fulton Burley later took over as the tenor and Betty Taylor had a long run as Slue Foot Sue.

42. The covered wagon was known as the Conestoga Wagon and it operated between 1955 and 1959.

43. Actor Don DeFore, who played George Baxter ("Mr. B.") on the *Hazel* (1961–1965) television series, used to own and operate a barbecue restaurant in Frontierland.

44. Annette Funicello made a special appearance for the show's 10,000th performance.

45. The *Mark Twain* riverboat is transformed to feature dozens of Disney characters celebrating the victory of good over evil at the conclusion of *Fantasmic!*

46. Country Bear Jamboree. He provided the voice for Big Al.

47. Guests descend on their five-story drop mirroring Brer Rabbit being thrown into the briar patch by Brer Fox.

48. The arcade is known as Teddi Barra's Swingin' Arcade. Teddi Barra is one of the entertainers featured in the Country Bear Jamboree.

49. The train station featured in the film *So Dear to My Heart* (1949) provided the inspiration for the New Orleans Square Railroad Station.

50. Cemeteries can also be found in three other attractions: Storybook Land Canal Boats, Frontierland Shootin' Arcade, and on Tom Sawyer Island.

Walt Disney World

Magic Kingdom

Questions:

1. Who conducted the 1,076-piece band on opening day of the Magic Kingdom?

2. What character is depicted in a bed of colorful flowers in front of the train station marking the entrance to the Magic Kingdom?

3. An engine named after which of Walt's Nine Old Men was introduced to the Walt Disney World Railroad in 1997?

4. What company sponsors a shop in the Town Square Exposition Hall?

5. Which classic nighttime parade returned to the Magic Kingdom beginning May 28, 1999?

6. True or false: Cinderella Castle can be taken apart in the event of a severe storm such as a hurricane.

7. From where in the Magic Kingdom does Tinker Bell begin her nightly flight?

8. How many mural panels make up the Cinderella Castle Mosaic?

9. What is the name of the restaurant located on the second floor of Cinderella Castle?

10. The Many Adventures of Winnie the Pooh replaced which Fantasyland attraction?

11. How many different themed rooms make up The Pinocchio Village Haus restaurant?

12. What is The Sword in the Stone Ceremony?

13. Which voice actor from the Pooh films was the only one to return to provide a special voice performance for the attraction's soundtrack in *The Many Adventures of Winnie the Pooh*?

14. What shape are the ride vehicles in The Many Adventures of Winnie the Pooh?

15. Which character runs the service garage located at Mickey's Toontown Fair?

16. According to chairman L. C. Clench of X-S Tech in The ExtraTERRORestrial Alien Encounter, what is the motto of their company?

17. What is the name of the cyberbotic performance unit (robot) that explains to guests how X-S Tech's new Teleportation system works in The ExtraTERRORestrial Alien Encounter?

18. What is the name of the science center building which houses The Timekeeper?

19. In The Timekeeper, which famous author is transported through history?

20. According to Tomorrowland's resident performer, Sonny Eclipse, what planet is he from?

21. What type of instrument does Sonny Eclipse play for guests at Cosmic Ray's Starlight Cafe?

22. Which Tomorrowland attraction includes a piece by legendary conductor/composer John Philip Sousa?

23. Which author/actor serves as the narrator in Walt Disney's Carousel of Progress?

24. To what was the name of the Grand Prix Raceway officially changed in 1996?

25. Take Flight was replaced in 1998 by what new attraction?

26. Which attraction is described by its slogan, "Sail with the wildest crew that ever sacked the Spanish Main"?

27. Which major attraction opened on December 15, 1973, the anniversary of Walt Disney's death?

28. The building that houses the Pirates of the Caribbean was inspired by what famous fortress in the Caribbean?

29. In Pirates of the Caribbean we see an individual being lowered into a well by a group of pirates. What office does the poor captive hold?

30. What kind of animal holds the keys to the prison cell where a band of pirates is being held in Pirates of the Caribbean?

31. What is the name of the attraction at the exit of the Jungle Cruise which allows guests the opportunity of piloting their own miniature versions of the Jungle Cruise boats?

32. According to the Jungle Cruise skippers, the falls known as Schweitzer Falls are named after whom?

33. What is the name of the attraction "owned" by Iago and Zazu?

34. The names of Iago and Zazu's Hollywood agents, William and Morris, to whom guests are introduced in the attraction's preshow queue area, are a parodic reference to what?

35. What is the name of the Tiki goddess Iago manages to upset?

36. What are the *Becky Thatcher, Huck Finn, Tom Sawyer,* and *Injun Joe*?

37. What is the name of the fort located on Tom Sawyer Island?

38. Which attraction is referred to as "the wildest show in the wilderness"?

39. Which bear in the Country Bear Jamboree is named after a state?

40. Name three of the instruments the Five Bear Rugs play in the Country Bear Jamboree.

41. According to Henry, what city is the rather large singer and performer Trixie from in the Country Bear Jamboree?

42. They are referred to as "those little sunbonnets from the Sunshine State" in the Country Bear Jamboree. Name the three performing bears.

43. Which attraction encourages guests to "Climb aboard 'n' hang on for the wildest ride in the wilderness"?

44. In which attraction can guests hear the songs "Ev'rybody Has a Laughing Place" and "How Do You Do"?

45. The Mile Long Bar and Pecos Bill Restaurant were merged and combined in 1998 to form what new restaurant?

46. What Liberty Square attraction was originally intended for Disneyland and was to be called One Nation Under God?

47. What Liberty Square restaurant was originally designed and planned for Disneyland?

48. What attraction features replicas of chess pieces located on its building's roof?

49. In 1989, a replica of what famous bell was added to Liberty Square?

50. The Silversmith and Olde World Antiques closed and reopened as what new merchandise shop?

Magic Kingdom

Answers:

1. Meredith Willson was band leader on opening day for the 1,076-piece band that marched up Main Street, U.S.A., playing his song "Seventy-Six Trombones." Willson is best remembered for composing such musicals as *The Music Man* and *The Unsinkable Molly Brown*.

2. Mickey Mouse is depicted in a bed of colorful flowers at the entrance to the Magic Kingdom.

3. In March 1997 the *Ward Kimball* joined the Walt Disney World Railroad. The *Ward Kimball* is engine number 5. It was built by the Davenport Locomotive Works in Davenport, Iowa in 1927.

4. The Eastman Kodak Camera Center reopened in 1998 and became the Town Square Exposition Hall/Camera Center. The new facility salutes the history and progress of photography and imagery.

5. The Main Street Electrical Parade with its more than 500,000 twinkling lights returned to entertain guests at the Magic Kingdom. The parade floats are actually those previously used in Disneyland. The former Walt Disney World version of the parade moved to Disneyland Paris at the time of the opening of the European park.

6. This is perhaps one of the most persistent myths that have surfaced over the years concerning the Magic Kingdom and, despite the many rumors, Cinderella Castle cannot be taken apart in the event of a severe storm.

7. Tinker Bell begins her nightly flight over the Magic Kingdom from Cinderella Castle.

8. A total of five mosaic murals can be found in the breezeway of Cinderella Castle. The panels depict scenes from the classic story "Cinderella." The mosaic tiles were all placed there by hand and over one million tiles make up the five murals. Each panel was designed by Disney artist Dorothea Redmond and then converted to Italian colored-glass mosaic pieces by Hanns-Joachin Scharff. A caricature of Disney Legend and Imagineer John Hench is featured within the mural's design.

9. In 1997, the restaurant's name was changed to Cinderella's Royal Table. Previously, the restaurant was known as King Stefan's Banquet Hall. Surprisingly, the character King Stefan is from the 1959 animated feature *Sleeping Beauty*, not from *Cinderella*.

10. Mr. Toad's Wild Ride, which closed on September 7, 1998.

11. The Pinocchio Village Haus restaurant is made up of seven themed rooms, each named after characters from the film. The different room names are: Blue Fairy, Cleo, Figaro, Jiminy Cricket, Monstro, Stromboli, and Geppetto's Workshop.

12. Each day a child is chosen by Merlin, the wizard from the animated feature *The Sword in the Stone*, to pull the sword from the stone and to be "Ruler of the Realm." The sword is embedded in a stone in front of Cinderella's Golden Carrousel.

13. Paul Winchell, the original voice of Tigger, provided a special performance of the character for the attraction's soundtrack.

14. The ride vehicles are shaped like oversized hunny pots.

15. Pete runs the service garage at Mickey's Toontown Fair.

16. X-S Tech's motto is "Seize the future."

17. The robot's name is S.I.R., which is short for Simulated Intelligence Robotics.

18. The official name of the building is the Metropolis Science Center.

19. Author Jules Verne is transported through history and into the future with the help of The Timekeeper.

20. The lounge singer Sonny Eclipse, who performs daily at Cosmic Ray's Starlight Café, is from Yew Nork City on the planet Zork.

21. Sonny refers to his musical instrument as the Amazing Astro Organ.

22. A rendition of John Philip Sousa's "Stars and Stripes Forever" can be heard in Walt Disney's Carousel of Progress.

23. Author/actor Jean Shepherd provides the voice of the *Audio-Animatronics*® figure, John, the show's narrator in Walt Disney's Carousel of Progress.

24. The Grand Prix Raceway officially changed its name to the Tomorrowland Speedway on September 28, 1996. On December 19,1999, it became the Tomorrowland Indy Speedway.

25. The new attraction is Buzz Lightyear's Space Ranger Spin. Guests move through a moving shooting gallery that allows them to use a joystick to spin their vehicles 360 degrees. Each vehicle is equipped with an interactive laser gun; when fired at a target it triggers animation, sound, or light and keeps a running score.

26. "Sail with the wildest crew that ever sacked the Spanish Main" is the slogan of the Pirates of the Caribbean.

27. Pirates of the Caribbean opened on December 15, 1973, the seventh anniversary of Walt Disney's death.

28. The famous fortress Castillo del Morro located in San Juan, Puerto Rico, provided designers with the inspiration for the building that houses the Pirates of the Caribbean.

29. The nasty pirates are lowering the town's mayor, Carlos, into the well in an effort to discover the whereabouts of a hidden treasure.

30. A dog curiously looks on, holding the keys to the cell in his mouth, while a group of imprisoned pirates try to convince him that he should pass them the keys.

31. Guests have the opportunity of piloting their own miniature versions of the Jungle Cruise boats at Shrunken Ned's Junior Jungle Boats.

32. Occasionally, the Jungle Cruise skippers will say the falls are named after the famous physician and humanitarian Dr. Albert Schweitzer. However, in most cases, in their constant effort to inject humor into the tour, they will say the falls are named after "Dr. Albert Falls."

33. According to the story, Iago and Zazu, because of their recent film notoriety, are the new owners of The Enchanted Tiki Room—Under New Management.

34. William and Morris' names refer to the famous William Morris Agency. Actor Don Rickles provides the voice of William, and the late Phil Hartman the voice of Morris.

35. Iago upsets the Tiki goddess Uh Oa.

36. These are the four rafts that transport guests over to Tom Sawyer Island.

37. On September 20, 1996, the fort located on Tom Sawyer Island had its name changed from Fort Clemens to Fort Langhorne. The name change was prompted by the release of the Walt Disney Pictures film *Tom and Huck* (1995), which featured a fort by that name.

38. "The wildest show in the wilderness" refers to the singing and entertaining bears of the Country Bear Jamboree.

39. Tennessee.

40. Zeke plays the banjo and a dishpan with his feet, Zeb plays the fiddle with a crooked hickory bow, Ted plays the corn jug and washboard, Fred plays the mouth harp and Tennessee plays the phang, which is described in the song as "just like a gi-tar but it's only got one strang."

41. According to your host, Henry, Trixie is "a special treat out of Tampa."

42. "Those little sunbonnets from the Sunshine State" are Bunny, Bubbles, and Beulah.

43. "Climb aboard 'n' hang on for the wildest ride in the wilderness" refers to the Big Thunder Mountain Railroad.

44. Splash Mountain. The two songs are from the 1946 Disney film *Song of the South*, which provided the inspiration for the attraction.

45. The new restaurant is known as Pecos Bill Tall Tale Inn and Cafe. The restaurant's story line is that Bill decided to open his own "waterin' hole" with his legendary friends' encouragement, and that as time went by those same friends visited his restaurant and left mementos behind for Bill, such as Paul Bunyan's ax, John Henry's hammer, and Annie Oakley's six-shooters. As a way of expressing his thanks, the famous cowboy then decided to decorate the walls of his restaurant with the items.

46. The Hall of Presidents.

47. The Columbia Harbor House was originally designed and planned for Disneyland and it was to overlook the harbor where the sailing ship *Columbia* carried guests around Tom Sawyer Island. However, plans changed and the restaurant, which opened in June 1972, was built at the Walt Disney World Magic Kingdom.

48. On the rooftop and turrets of the Haunted Mansion are replicas of chess pieces such as rooks, pawns, kings, and queens.

49. In 1989, a replica of the actual Liberty Bell was specially cast for the Walt Disney World Resort and placed in Liberty Square.

50. Ye Olde Christmas Shoppe.

Epcot-Future World

Questions:

1. In which Future World attraction can guests see a depiction of Sophocles' play *Oedipus Rex* being performed?

2. Name one of the two Future World merchandise shops located at the base of Spaceship Earth.

3. Which famous Disney songwriting team wrote the theme song for the short-lived Future World attraction the Astuter Computer Revue?

4. Name one of the Future World attractions closed to make room for the opening of Innoventions in 1994.

5. A life-size *Audio-Animatronics*® figure of what actress/comedian is featured in the Universe of Energy?

6. In *Ellen's Energy Adventure*, who helps educate Ellen DeGeneres on the history and uses of energy?

7. Which popular actor plays the part of the stomach in Cranium Command?

8. Which two actors play the parts of the heart in Cranium Command?

9. Which Future World pavilion was originally going to be called the Century 3 pavilion?

10. Which Future World pavilion officially closed on January 9, 1999?

11. Which former Future World attraction featured the theme song "It's Fun to Be Free"?

12. Which Future World attraction's vehicles are controlled by three onboard computers which together have more processing power than the Space Shuttle?

13. Which famous race car driver, who is associated with the Walt Disney World Speedway, helped dedicate Test Track for its grand opening on March 17, 1999?

14. Who were Fuzzball, Hooter, the Geex, and Major and Minor Domo?

15. What is the name of the organization that honors Prof. Wayne Szalinski with its Inventor of the Year Award in *Honey, I Shrunk the Audience*?

16. What actor portrays the chairman of the organization that presents Prof. Wayne Szalinski his award in *Honey, I Shrunk the Audience*?

17. The Land is located between which two Future World pavilions?

18. The original design concept for The Land was eventually used as the inspiration for a science project based in what state?

19. What attraction features performers named Chubby Cheddar, Neil Moussaka, and the Got-the-Point Sisters?

20. What is the name of the merchandise shop that replaced the Centorium in 1999?

Epcot-Future World

Answers:

1. As guests travel through Spaceship Earth they experience a scene depicting a Greek theater where Audio-Animatronics® characters are performing a scene from Sophocles' play *Oedipus Rex*. The play, written by Sophocles around 428 B.C., is considered one of the three greatest extant tragedies of ancient Greek theater.

2. Gateway Gifts or Camera Center.

3. Robert and Richard Sherman wrote the theme song for the Astuter Computer Revue. The attraction was designed to explain the inner workings of computers by utilizing animation and the computers used to operate many of the Epcot attractions. The attraction was only open briefly, from October 1, 1982, to January 2, 1984.

4. The technology display area, Innoventions, occupies the site which formally housed FutureCom, Energy Exchange, Epcot Outreach, Epcot Computer Central, and Epcot Teacher's Center.

5. Ellen DeGeneres.

6. Bill Nye, known for his syndicated television show *Bill Nye, the Science Guy*, helps educate Ellen on the history and uses of energy.

7. Actor George Wentz plays the stomach that always seems to be hungry. Wentz may best be remembered for playing the part of Norm on the long-running television comedy *Cheers* (1982–1993).

8. Actors Dana Carvey and Kevin Nealon reprise their familiar *Saturday Night Live* Hans and Franz routine as they play the parts of the heart in Cranium Command.

9. Horizons was originally going to be called the Century 3 pavilion. It was designed to celebrate the envisioned technological achievements of America's third century, the years of the 21st century leading up to the U.S. Tricentennial in 2076 and what those advances will mean to our everyday lives.

10. Horizons.

11. "It's Fun to Be Free" was the theme song for the former Future World attraction World of Motion.

12. Amazingly enough, the Test Track vehicles with their three onboard computers have more processing power than the Space Shuttle.

13. Legendary race car driver Richard Petty helped dedicate Test Track. On hand helping Petty were supermodels Christie Brinkley, Carol Alt, Angie Everhart, and Frederica. The Richard Petty Driving Experience at the Walt Disney World Speedway offers qualified guests a high-speed driving experience.

14. They were Captain Eo's crew members in the 3-D film by that same name.

15. The organization's name is the Imagination Institute.

16. The chairman of the Imagination Institute is Dr. Nigel Channing, played by actor Eric Idle.

17. The Land is located between Imagination and The Living Seas.

18. The original design concept for The Land provided the inspiration for Biosphere II, the famous enclosed ecosystem project in Arizona.

19. The attraction Food Rocks features entertaining parodies of such musical performers as Chubby Checker, Neil Sedaka, and the Pointer Sisters.

20. The new merchandise shop is Mouse Gear, which opened in 1999 to coincide with the fifteen-month Walt Disney World millennium celebration at Epcot.

Epcot-World Showcase

1. The double-decker buses that used to circle the World Showcase Lagoon each were named after a different world city. Name two of the six cities that the buses were named after.

2. Which World Showcase restaurant resembles a castle?

3. Why is the amphitheater located across from The American Adventure referred to as the America Gardens Theatre?

4. Which attraction includes the songs "Golden Dreams," "Two Brothers," and "Brother, Can You Spare a Dime"?

5. Why is The American Adventure building actually larger in height- and design than any of the other buildings in World Showcase?

6. Which World Showcase country was the only one where a large contingency of workers were brought from that nation to help work on the intricate architectural details of the pavilion?

7. Which famous Paris waterway is depicted in France?

8. What is the translation of *Otium cum Dignitate,* the motto of the Rose and Crown Pub at the United Kingdom?

9. The building that houses the merchandise shop known as The Tea Caddy in the United Kingdom resembles what famous cottage located in the English town of Stratford-Upon-Avon?

10. What new pavilion was added to World Showcase in 1999 to help commemorate the year 2000?

Epcot-World Showcase

Answers:

1. The six cities were Berlin, London, Paris, Peking, Toronto, and Marrakesh.
2. Restaurant Akershus, located in Norway, was inspired by the magnificent castle of Akershus, overlooking Oslo harbor. The restaurant strives to bring guests the freshest and most up-to-date authentic Norwegian foods and culinary trends.
3. The amphitheater has a collection of live trees and plants located throughout its seating area.
4. The songs are featured in The American Adventure.
5. Walt Disney Imagineers used a process known as inverted forced perspective on The American Adventure because they discovered that a building from that time period would have been too small to be seen across the World Showcase Lagoon.
6. Morocco.
7. As guests approach France they walk over a footbridge inspired by the Pont des Artes, which at one point was located over the Seine River in Paris.
8. The motto of the Rose and Crown Pub is expressed on a sign out front, *Otium cum Dignitate,* which translates from Latin as "leisure with dignity."
9. The building was designed to resemble Ann Hathaway's cottage located in Stratford-Upon-Avon. Hathaway was the wife of playwright William Shakespeare. Interestingly, the United Kingdom is a blending of different architectural styles through four-hundred years of British history. As guests proceed up the streets of the United Kingdom away from the World Showcase Lagoon, the building styles advance chronologically from Shakespeare's time (1500s) to the age of the Victorians (1800s).
10. The Millennium Village was added to World Showcase to help commemorate the year 2000. The pavilion was designed to give a collection of nations, not currently represented at Epcot, a chance to share their unique cultural identities. Guests have the opportunity, for example, of walking through a Brazilian rain forest, experiencing firsthand the four seasons of Sweden, and meeting artisans from around the world.

Disney-MGM Studios

Questions:

1. Which Disney executive presided over the dedication of the Disney-MGM Studios?

2. What actor hosted the television special *The Disney-MGM Studios Theme Park Grand Opening,* which appeared on ABC?

3. What former California auditorium provided the inspiration for the park's entrance?

4. Where at the Disney-MGM Studios can one find the Crossroads of the World structure?

5. What former Disney-MGM Studios parade was inspired by a 1992 full-length animated feature?

6. On April 30, 1927, legendary film stars Mary Pickford and Douglas Fairbanks participated in a ceremony that is re-created at the Disney-MGM Studios in front of the Chinese Theater. What is this ceremony?

7. What is the significance behind the license plate number "021-429" on the car depicted in the gangster shoot-out sequence of The Great Movie Ride?

8. An *Audio-Animatronics*® figure of actor James Cagney is featured in which attraction?

9. What is so unique about the plane featured in one of the scenes of The Great Movie Ride?

10. SuperStar Television closed in 1998 only to reopen in 1999 as what new attraction?

11. The Monster Sound Show was replaced in 1997 by what attraction?

12. What popular television actor plays detective Charlie Foster in the attraction *Sounds Dangerous*?

13. True or false: one of the original concepts for the park was a stunt show based on the James Bond character and films.

14. What name appears as the manufacturer on the television sets featured in the '50s Prime Time Cafe?

15. The Studio Commissary changed its name to what in 1997?

16. What are the names of the two hecklers located in the box seats of *Muppet*Vision 3D*?

17. Why is the boarding announcement in Star Tours for an "Egroeg Sacul" so appropriate?

18. What prop from the 1984 Touchstone Pictures film *Splash* is on display on Mickey Avenue?

19. The Sunset Market Ranch was inspired by which popular Los Angeles landmark?

20. Where is the "Home of the Victory Dog"?

21. Which nighttime spectacular, starring Mickey Mouse, officially opened to studio guests on October 15, 1998?

22. Which evil creature confronts Mickey at the conclusion of Fantasmic!?

23. What musical instrument dominates the building's facade marking the entrance to Rock 'n' Roller Coaster starring Aerosmith?

24. What is the name of the fictitious recording company located in Rock 'n' Roller Coaster starring Aerosmith?

25. What is the name of the merchandise shop that replaced Endor Vendors?

Disney-MGM Studios

Answers:

1. On May 1, 1989, Disney CEO and chairman Michael Eisner officially presided over the dedication of the Disney-MGM Studios.

2. Actor John Ritter, star of the hit television comedy series *Three's Company* (1977–1984), hosted the Disney special.

3. The Pan Pacific Auditorium, which served as a Southern California landmark from 1935–1972, provided Disney Imagineers with the inspiration for the park's entrance. The original structure was designed by the architectural teams of Walter Wurdeman and Welton Becket. Interestingly, Becket was a friend and neighbor of Walt Disney's, and had convinced him to plan his Disneyland park in-house rather than go to outside architects.

4. The Crossroads of the World structure is an icon located at the start of Hollywood Boulevard at the entrance to the park. It features Mickey Mouse on top of a globe, and is based on a similar structure in Hollywood, California.

5. The 1992 animated feature *Aladdin* provided the inspiration for the Aladdin's Royal Caravan parade.

6. Film stars Mary Pickford and Douglas Fairbanks were the first couple to place their hands and footprints into the cement outside Grauman's Chinese Theater on Hollywood Boulevard. The ceremony is repeated at the Disney-MGM Studios from time to time throughout the year to honor the stars of today.

7. The license plate number "021-429" represents the date, February 14, 1929, on which the infamous St. Valentine's Day Massacre occurred in Chicago, Illinois.

8. An *Audio-Animatronics*® figure of James Cagney is depicted in a scene from the 1931 motion picture *The Public Enemy* in The Great Movie Ride.

9. The plane is featured in the *Casablanca* show scene of The Great Movie Ride. The plane in the background is the actual plane used in the classic film *Casablanca* (1942).

10. On March 15, 1999, the musical stage show *Disney's Doug Live!* opened at the Disney-MGM Studios. The show combines live actors, animation, and revolving stages in a thirty-minute performance that is shown several times each day.

11. *One Saturday Morning,* based on the ABC television series, which was in turn replaced in 1999 by *Sounds Dangerous.*

12. *Sounds Dangerous* is featured at the ABC Sound Studio and it stars Drew Carey (from television's *The Drew Carey Show*). Carey plays detective Charlie Foster in the twelve-minute sound show experience, which features the first use of binaural sound in a 250-seat theater.

13. True. One of the original concepts for the park was a stunt show based on the popular James Bond character and films. It was eventually decided a stunt show based on Indiana Jones would work better.

14. Disney.

15. The Studio Commissary changed its name to the ABC Commissary. The name changed shortly after the purchase of ABC/Capital Cities by The Walt Disney Company.

16. The two familiar hecklers are Waldorf and Statler, characters from the *Muppet* series.

17. The reference to a "Egroeg Sacul" is actually a clever salute to the creator of the *Star Wars* films. Spell it backwards and it becomes George Lucas.

18. At the one end of Mickey Avenue is the actual mermaid fountain that Madison presented to Allen Bauer in the film *Splash* (1984).

19. Since 1934, the famous Farmers Market, located at 3rd and Fairfax, has been a popular hangout for Angelenos and visitors alike, and the Sunset Market Ranch is based on it.

20. The "Home of the Victory Dog" describes the Sunset Boulevard food location Rosie's All-American Cafe. Rosie is a reference to the World War II character "Rosie the Riveter" and since the theme for Sunset Boulevard is the 1930s and 1940s, the name is appropriate.

21. October 15, 1998, officially marked the debut of the nighttime spectacular *Fantasmic!*

22. Maleficent, after she has transformed herself into a fire-breathing dragon, confronts Mickey at the conclusion of *Fantasmic!*

23. A forty-five-foot-tall electric guitar dominates the entrance to Rock 'n' Roller Coaster starring Aerosmith.

24. The fictitious company is known as G-Force Recording Company. According to the story, the company was established during the heyday of Hollywood in the 1930s.

25. On September 15, 1999, Tatooine Traders, the new merchandise shop themed after the film *Star Wars: Episode 1—The Phantom Menace*, opened at the Disney-MGM Studios.

Disney's Animal Kingdom

Questions:

1. On what date did the park officially open?

2. The main icon for Disney's Animal Kingdom is the Tree of Life. How high does the Tree of Life stand—40, 145, 200, or 250 feet?

3. What materials were used to construct the Tree of Life?

4. What is the name of the tropical garden area filled with exotic plants and animals that guests first discover as they enter the park?

5. Where is the 3-D film *It's Tough to Be a Bug!* shown?

6. Who is the host for the 3-D film *It's Tough to Be a Bug!?*

7. The story line for the Tree of Life is that one day a little ant planted a seed and wished for a tree to grow to protect him and all the animals that lived in that area. On what was barren land, a tree eventually grew. The little ant and the rest of the colony along with a collection of other little insects formed a theater group and began to produce stage shows. What is the name of the theater group they formed?

8. What is the name of the bridge that marks the entrance to Dinoland U.S.A.?

9. According to the story line, how many million years do guests travel back in Countdown to Extinction?

10. What is the name of the organization that enables guests to travel back in time in Countdown to Extinction?

11. What is the name of the organization's director and what is its motto in Countdown to Extinction?

12. What are the names of the vehicles that transport guests on their journey into the past in Countdown to Extinction?

13. Countdown to Extinction uses the same ride technology as which attraction at Disneyland?

14. What is the name of the children's play area located in Dinoland U.S.A.?

15. What was the first themed "land" to be added after the park's initial opening in 1998?

16. What is the name of the mythical kingdom guests enter when they visit the themed land of Asia?

17. When translated, what does the name of the mythical village located in Asia mean?

18. What is the name of the thrilling and breathtaking white-water raft ride located in Asia?

19. What is the name of the fictitious river that serves as the setting for the Kali River Rapids?

20. What is the name of the illegal logging company depicted in Kali River Rapids?

21. What is the name of the walking journey through the lush home of myriad animals and bird species in Asia?

22. As guests enter the themed "land" of Africa they enter a village by the name of Harambe, a realistic, contemporary representation of an East African coastal town poised on the edge of the 21st century where visitors are encouraged to eat, shop, and enjoy the unique village setting. What does the word *harambe* mean?

23. According to the story line, in what year did the Harambe Wilderness Reserve open?

24. What are the names of the warden and wildlife researcher who can be heard over the radio during the journey on the Kilimanjaro Safaris?

25. What kind of animal are Zari and Miles, the first two animals the new park welcomed?

26. Pangani Forest Exploration Trail was originally known by what other name when Disney's Animal Kingdom first opened?

27. What does the name *Pangani* mean?

28. What is the name of the railroad line that transports guests on their trek to Conservation Station?

29. Which New York mountain range was used as the inspiration for Camp Minnie-Mickey?

30. Which 1994 full-length animated feature inspired a live stage production performed daily?

Disney's Animal Kingdom

Answers:

1. Disney's Animal Kingdom officially opened on Earth Day, April 22, 1998. By 9:00 A.M. the park had to close due to capacity. The park had been announced and ground-breaking ceremonies took place in 1995.

2. The man-made Tree of Life stands 145 feet and it features over 325 images of animals, birds, and insects intricately carved on its roots and trunk.

3. The tree stands as the centerpiece of the park. It is covered with approximately 103,000 leaves, which are made of plastic. The branches are constructed of fiberglass and the trunk and roots are made from concrete. The fourteen-story creation is fifty feet wide at its trunk's base with roots that spread 170 feet in diameter. More than 8,000 branches make up the foliage that spreads 160 feet wide over the park.

4. The Oasis.

5. The 3-D film *It's Tough to Be a Bug!* is shown in a theater at the base of the Tree of Life, beneath its roots.

6. The ant Flik is the host of *It's Tough to Be a Bug!* The character is also the star of the 1998 animated film *A Bug's Life.*

7. The group is known as the Tree of Life Repertory Players.

8. The bridge is known as Oldengate Bridge. A 40-foot-tall Brachiosaurus skeleton has been reassembled to create this magnificent gateway.

9. According to the story line, guests travel 65 million years into the past to discover what life was like at the end of the Cretaceous period, when a giant meteor supposedly hit the Earth and led to the dinosaurs' extinction.

10. The organization is known as the Dino Institute.

11. Prior to boarding for their journey back in time, guests are shown a film featuring the organization's director, Dr. Helen Marsh, played by actress Phylicia Rashad. According to Dr. Marsh, the institute's motto is "The Future is in the Past." This is the second time Rashad has appeared in a Disney attraction preshow. Her first appearance was in the original Backstage Studio Tour, which featured Rashad in a short film about television production.

12. The vehicles are known as Time Rover vehicles.

13. Indiana Jones Adventure.

14. The children's play area is known as The Boneyard. Children get the opportunity to slither, climb, slide, and crawl through a dig site, and help uncover the remains of a woolly mammoth.

15. Asia, which opened on March 18, 1999, was the first themed land to be added to the park after its initial opening in 1998.

16. As guests cross the bridge to Asia, they enter the mythical Kingdom of Anandapur, filled with crumbling yet beautiful ruins of the ancient village, its temples, a maharajah's palace and a thrilling white-water raft ride. Guests soon discover a natural treasure of wild creatures while taking an unforgettable expedition.

17. Anandapur translates as "place of all delights."

18. The attraction is known as the Kali River Rapids. It propels guests on a turbulent, wild, and wet ride through a jungle habitat jeopardized by illegal logging.

19. The fictitious river is known as the Chakranadi River. Its name translates as "river that flows in a circle."

20. Tetak Logging Company. The word "tetak" means to chop.

21. The attraction is known as the Maharajah Jungle Trek, where guests discover such animals as tigers, Malayan tapirs, fruit bats, and even the largest lizard species in the world—the Komodo dragon. The area also features over fifty varieties of birds in the Aviary.

22. *Harambe* means "coming together" or "let's pull together" in Swahili.

23. According to the story line, the Harambe Wilderness Reserve, home of the Kilimanjaro Safaris, opened in 1971.

24. The warden is Wilson Mutua and the wildlife researcher is Dr. Catherine Jobson.

25. Zari and Miles are both giraffes. Zari, the female, was acquired from the Metro Washington Park Zoo in Portland, Oregon, and Miles, a male, was from the St. Louis Zoological Park.

26. Pangani Forest Exploration Trail was originally known as Gorilla Falls Exploration Trail. The name was changed to better represent the variety of animals that one may encounter while on the trail, such as hippopotamuses, meerkats, naked mole rats, and exotic birds.

27. *Pangani* means "place of enchantment" or "place of spirits."

28. The railroad line is known as the Eastern Star Railways. The train line consists of two trains, and each train has five cars pulled by one engine. There is a third engine that serves as a backup. The three engines and two sets of cars were constructed in Alchester, England, only a few miles from the cottage of William Shakespeare in Stratford-Upon-Avon.

29. Camp Minnie-Mickey re-creates an Adirondack Mountain resort, where the characters have gone on vacation.

30. The 1994 feature *The Lion King* provided the inspiration for the live stage production *Festival of the Lion King* performed daily at Camp Minnie-Mickey.

Tokyo
Disneyland

Questions:

1. Unlike the three other Magic Kingdom theme parks (Disneyland, Walt Disney World, and Disneyland Paris), the Tokyo Disneyland Railroad does not circle the entire park. Why?

2. What is the name of the nighttime parade spectacular featuring special effects and lasers at Tokyo Disneyland?

3. What is the name of the Fantasyland attraction inspired by the Winnie the Pooh stories?

4. What is the name of the Fantasyland restaurant that opened in 1998 and was inspired by the full-length animated feature *Alice in Wonderland* (1951)?

5. Which themed land opened April 15, 1996, to help commemorate the park's 13th anniversary?

6. What toylike device is featured on top of the Jolly Trolley?

7. What popular American songwriting team provided the music for the attraction Meet the World?

8. What is the name of the attraction based on the popular *Honey, I Shrunk the Kids* film series?

9. What is the name of the Tomorrowland attraction that is equivalent to the Walt Disney World Magic Kingdom attraction The Timekeeper?

10. Name the first Disney-brand resort to be built at Tokyo Disneyland.

Tokyo
Disneyland

Answers:

1. The Tokyo Disneyland Railroad doesn't circle the entire park because under Japanese law if the track were any longer than it is, it would be classified as a public utility and fall under the jurisdiction of the government.
2. The nighttime parade is known as Fantillusion!
3. Pooh's Honey Hunt.
4. Inspired by the feature film Alice in Wonderland (1951) is the Queen of Hearts Banquet Hall. It is the first Tokyo Disneyland restaurant to feature onstage food preparation.
5. On April 15, 1996, Tokyo Disneyland opened its seventh themed land, Mickey's Toontown.
6. The toylike device on top of the Jolly Trolley is a wind-up key.
7. The Sherman brothers.
8. The attraction, which opened on April 15, 1997, to commemorate the park's 14th anniversary, is known as *MicroAdventure!* Imagineers exported the design of the popular *Honey, I Shrunk the Audience* attraction from Epcot to Japan. The new attraction features revised special effects along with a new sequence shot specifically for the Japanese audience.
9. Visionarium. It is based on an attraction that was created for Disneyland Paris.
10. In the summer of 2000, the 6-story 504-room Disney Ambassador Hotel is scheduled to open.

Disneyland Paris

Questions:

1. In which French city is Disneyland Paris located?

2. Which restaurant displays props and paintings used as inspiration for the different themed lands of Disneyland Paris?

3. What is the street address of Walt's—an American Restaurant?

4. In commemoration of the park's fifth anniversary in 1997, what was the castle temporarily redesigned to resemble?

5. What shape are the ride vehicles in the Fantasyland Ferris wheel, Les Pirouettes du Vieux Moulin?

6. What attraction features references to the stories of "Hansel and Gretel" and "The Wizard of Oz"?

7. What attraction features a cameo appearance by French actor Gérard Depardieu?

8. What is the only Discoveryland attraction you can walk through while others ride?

9. What are the ride vehicles called in Space Mountain—De la Terre á la Lune?

10. Which Disney television show inspired the futuristic look of Autopia?

11. What is the name of the entertainment complex located within Discoveryland that features live stage shows, bands, and dancing in a technologically sophisticated discotheque?

12. Which Frontierland attraction was inspired by a 1995 full-length animated feature?

13. Which three Disney adventure films provided the inspiration for Adventure Isle?

14. What shape are the ride vehicles in Indiana Jones™ et le Temple du Péril?

15. Where can one find a large egg on top of a building?

Disneyland Paris

Answers:

1. The French city Marne-la-Vallée is home to Disneyland Paris.

2. Located on the second floor of Walt's—an American Restaurant are props and artwork used by Disney Imagineers as their inspiration for the different themed lands of Disneyland Paris.

3. The address is 1401 Flower Street, a clever salute to the location of the headquarters of Walt Disney Imagineering in Glendale, California.

4. To mark the occasion, the castle was renamed "The Castle of Fools" to coincide with the release of the full-length animated feature *The Hunchback of Notre Dame*. The castle was topped off with a 39-foot jester's hat.

5. Guests ride in vehicles that resemble water buckets.

6. Hansel and Gretel's cottage and the Emerald City from "The Wizard of Oz" are featured in Le Pays des Contes de Fées, which is patterned after the Storybook Land Canal Boats found in Disneyland.

7. Actor Gérard Depardieu makes a cameo appearance in Le Visionarium.

8. Space Mountain—De la Terre á la Lune has been designed to allow guests the opportunity of walking through the attraction while watching others ride.

9. The ride vehicles are referred to as Rocket Trains. They blast guests up five stories to start an exciting ride through the solar system.

10. The futuristic cars featured in the Autopia attraction are inspired by the 1958 Disney television show *Magic Highway U.S.A.*, which showed America's highways from their earliest days to the highways of the future.

11. Videopolis.

12. Pocahontas Indian Village.

13. The three Disney films that provided the inspiration for Adventure Isle are *Treasure Island* (1950), *Peter Pan* (1953), and *Swiss Family Robinson* (1960).

14. Guests board rickety-looking ore cars and are transported into the heart of an ancient ruined temple.

15. Among the many stories that influenced the development of
    Adventureland are the Sinbad tales. In one of the stories, Sinbad
    confronts the large mythical roc bird. As a tribute to Sinbad, a large
    egg from the roc is featured on one of the Adventureland buildings.

Theme Park Potpourri

Questions:

1. Which former U.S. Navy officer was coaxed out of retirement by Walt Disney to direct the construction of Disneyland park?

2. Why was opening day at Disneyland, July 17, 1955, referred to as "Black Sunday"?

3. For which park were both a Liberty Street and an Edison Square planned?

4. Originally, what was Adventureland going to be named?

5. Who was the first United States president to visit Disneyland?

6. From which organization did Walt Disney borrow character costumes for the opening of Disneyland?

7. How many attractions were *E* ticket rides when the letter tickets were first introduced at Disneyland in 1955?

8. What was Hobbyland?

9. Which vice president of the United States presided over the opening day ceremonies for the Monorail at Disneyland?

10. Which former U.S. Army officer was asked to lead the effort to transform Florida swampland into a site for the Magic Kingdom?

11. Where was the Walt Disney World Preview Center located?

12. What was Walt Disney World originally going to be named?

13. What was the name of a major proposed Walt Disney World Magic Kingdom attraction, designed by the late Disney legend Marc Davis, which told a humorous tale of American cowboys and Mexican gauchos through the use of *Audio-Animatronics*®?

14. What is a "dark ride"?

15. What is the name of the band comprised of college students from around the country that entertains guests during the summer season at Disneyland and Walt Disney World?

16. Disneyland and the Walt Disney World Magic Kingdom are open late during selected days in the spring to recognize graduating high school seniors. What are these special nights known as?

17. Which was the first Disney theme park not dedicated by a Disney family member?

18. Prior to the construction of Epcot, the entrance had to be moved 300 feet to help save what endangered animal— woodpecker, alligator, or snail darter?

19. How many attractions were in operation when Epcot opened on October 1, 1982—16, 19, 26, or 48?

20. True or false: one of the early concepts for Epcot called for all of the attractions of Future World and World Showcase to be housed in one building.

21. Prior to 1984, which two days of the week was Disneyland closed?

22. The inspiration for the Disney-MGM Studios came from a pavilion suggested for which other theme park?

23. In which of the four Magic Kingdom theme parks did Splash Mountain open first?

24. What was the name of the sophisticated holiday musical that has been performed at Disneyland, based on a Tchaikovsky ballet?

25. Which was the first European theme park to open 365 days a year?

26. Which was the first Disney high-speed attraction to have an onboard synchronized musical soundtrack?

27. How many different monorails comprise the Disneyland fleet of monorails?

28. Of the four Magic Kingdoms, which one features the most attractions and shows?

29. Where was the first Preview Center ever to promote the opening of a single attraction?

30. Which month of the year has seen the opening of more Disney theme parks than any other?

31. What was the original name used to describe Disney's Animal Kingdom?

32. True or false: Walt Disney World Resort has a fleet of ships that makes it the seventh largest Navy in the world.

33. How many different monorails comprise the Walt Disney World fleet?

34. Which Disneyland themed land features foliage and plants that are edible?

35. Which was the first Disney theme park where guests could create their own CDs featuring the music, narration, and sounds of the parks?

36. Where is the largest outdoor theater at the Walt Disney World Resort located?

37. Where in the U.S. can you find the most people working for one company, all in one location?

38. Of the four theme parks that comprise the Walt Disney World Resort, how many feature attractions with either evidence of dinosaur remains or dinosaurs themselves?

39. What is the fastest Disney attraction featured in any theme park?

40. What is the first attraction at Walt Disney World to feature a high-speed launch and multiple complete inversions?

Theme Park Potpourri

....

Answers:

1. Walt Disney coaxed Rear Admiral Joseph "Joe" Fowler to supervise the construction of Disneyland. Fowler was later asked by Roy O. Disney to lead the effort to build Walt Disney World.

2. The opening day at Disneyland, July 17, 1955, was referred to as "Black Sunday" because of all the opening day problems the park experienced, from plumbing to overall operational mishaps. The nickname was a reference to "Black Monday," the day of the October 29, 1929, stock market crash.

3. Disneyland. Liberty Street and Edison Square were both themed lands featured on the very first map of the park. Liberty Street was to be a Colonial-themed area honoring America's heritage and Edison Square saluted a turn-of-the-century celebration of electricity. Neither area was built at Disneyland, but the concept of Liberty Street was resurrected to become the basis of its own themed land at the Walt Disney World Magic Kingdom.

4. Adventureland was originally going to be called True-Life Adventureland after the successful True-Life Adventure film series produced by the company.

5. Harry S. Truman was the first president to visit Disneyland though his visit took place after his term. Interestingly, Ronald Reagan, later to reach the highest office, was on hand during opening day ceremonies.

6. Time and budgets did not permit the development of character costumes by the company when Disneyland opened. So Walt Disney had to borrow costumes from the Ice Capades, which had created them for one of its shows.

7. None. The first ticket books had only A, B, and C tickets. The E tickets were not introduced until 1959.

8. Hobbyland was a short-lived themed area in the early days of Disneyland featuring various model kits.

9. Vice President Richard M. Nixon presided over the opening of the Monorail on June 14, 1959. The Disneyland Monorail became the first monorail in North America. It also became the first such system to cross over a public street with its extension to the Disneyland Hotel in 1961.

10. Major General William E. "Joe" Potter supervised the transformation of 300 acres of Florida swampland into a site for the Magic Kingdom. He had at one time served as governor of the Panama Canal Zone.

11. In January 1970, the Walt Disney World Preview Center opened at Lake Buena Vista. Tour Guides used artists' renderings, slides, and a film to educate guests about the upcoming Walt Disney World. More than one million guests visited the center.

12. Walt Disney World was simply going to be called Disney World. It was Roy O. Disney who insisted that the project be named after Walt because it was inspired by his brother's dreams.

13. The attraction was to be known as the Western River Expedition. A model for it was displayed for several years in the Walt Disney Story attraction.

14. A "dark ride" places a guest in a windowless building and makes extensive use of black light (ultraviolet light), which when used in specially painted scenes, makes them glow as if by magic. Peter Pan's Flight, Snow White's Scary Adventures, Roger Rabbit's Car Toon Spin, and The Many Adventures of Winnie the Pooh are some of the attractions referred to as "dark rides."

15. Since 1971 at Disneyland and 1972 at Walt Disney World, the Collegiate All-Star Band has entertained guests with an array of music including rock, jazz, and Disney songs. It was originally called the All-American College Band.

16. For many years, Disneyland and Walt Disney World have hosted "Grad Nites" to recognize graduating high school seniors with their own special night in the park.

17. On October 24, 1982, Epcot was officially dedicated by Disney chairman and CEO E. Cardon "Card" Walker. Disneyland and Walt Disney World were dedicated by Walt Disney and Roy O. Disney, respectively.

18. A project team discovered a red-cockaded woodpecker nesting in the area. Recognizing the bird as endangered, the team moved the site to preserve the nesting area in its natural state. In honor of the bird, a back service road was given the name Woodpecker Road.

19. Nineteen: Future World consisted of fourteen opening-day attractions and World Showcase had five.

20. True. One of the early concepts for Epcot featured all of the attractions under one roof.

21. Disneyland used to be closed on Mondays and Tuesdays during the off-seasons. Soon after Michael Eisner took over the top spot of The Walt Disney Company, he made the change and established a seven-day operating week for Disneyland year-round.

22. Disney designers had explored the possibility of opening a pavilion based on the movies at Epcot. During the planning, it was decided that the pavilion would work better as its own theme park.

23. Splash Mountain opened first in Disneyland on the park's anniversary, July 17, 1989, followed by openings in the Walt Disney World Magic Kingdom, Tokyo Disneyland, and Disneyland Paris.

24. Mickey's Nutcracker.

25. Disneyland Paris was the first European theme park to open 365 days a year.

26. Space Mountain at Disneyland was equipped with a synchronized musical soundtrack in 1996, a first for any Disney attraction.

27. There are four monorails that comprise the Disneyland Mark V fleet. Each is designated by a different color: purple, orange, blue, and red.

28. Disneyland features over sixty attractions and shows.

29. The Preview Center promoting Test Track was the first such center and exhibit spotlighting the opening of a single attraction. Historically, preview centers are constructed to promote and advertise the opening of an entire theme park, such as Epcot and Disney's California Adventure.

30. April, with three: Tokyo Disneyland (1983), Disneyland Paris (1992), and Disney's Animal Kingdom (1998).

31. Originally the name of the park was going to be Disney's Wild Animal Kingdom. The word "Wild" was dropped because company officials wanted to avoid confusion with the television show *Mutual of Omaha's Wild Kingdom* (1963–1971).

32. True. Remarkably, the Walt Disney World Resort does have a fleet of ships that makes it the seventh largest Navy in the world. Please don't look to this fleet for national defense unless your needs include pontoon boats, speedboats, rafts, a riverboat, and several ferries.

33. There are twelve monorails that comprise the Walt Disney World Mark VI fleet. Each is designated by a different color: Red, Black, Blue, Gold, Orange, Green, Purple, Pink, Coral, Lime, Silver, and Yellow. They travel on 13.7 miles of monorail beam and transport on average 150,000 guests per day. The entire monorail fleet travels an estimated 7 million miles each year.

34. In 1998, with the opening of New Tomorrowland, a unique feature was added to the land's foliage and plants—they are edible! Some of the new plants include coffee plants, and avocado and orange trees.

35. When New Tomorrowland opened in 1998 at Disneyland, a facility known as "Disneyland Forever" gave guests the opportunity to create their own CDs, incorporating the sounds of the park.

36. The Hollywood Hills Amphitheater located at the Disney-MGM Studios is the largest theater on the property. The facility plays host to the nighttime spectacular *Fantasmic!* with 6,900 seats and standing room for an additional 3,000 people.

37. Since 1998, Walt Disney World.

38. All four parks have references to dinosaurs. Dinosaur remains are shown unearthed at the Big Thunder Mountain Railroad. Epcot features dinosaurs inside the Universe of Energy. Gertie the Dinosaur is located at Echo Lake at the Disney-MGM Studios and Disney's Animal Kingdom is the home of Dinoland U.S.A.

39. The fastest attraction is Test Track located at Epcot. The attraction, which opened in 1999, reaches speeds of 65 mph.

40. Located on Sunset Boulevard at the Disney-MGM Studios is Rock 'n' Roller Coaster starring Aerosmith, the first Walt Disney World attraction to feature both a high-speed launch and multiple complete inversions. The twists and turns of the attraction are intensified by a synchronized rock soundtrack resonating from speakers mounted in each vehicle.

Disney Resorts/
Other
Attractions

....

Questions:

1. The first monorail trains that transported guests at Disneyland were constructed where?

2. Which Disney resort was originally referred to as the Tempo Bay Resort Hotel?

3. Early in its construction, what company owned Disney's Contemporary Resort?

4. What were the Venetian, Mediterranean, Asian, and Persian Resorts?

5. Which Disney artist was responsible for the 90-foot-tall mural featured in the main building of Disney's Contemporary Resort?

6. Which Walt Disney World resort's motto is Aita Peatea?

7. What famous seventeenth-century palace provided the inspiration for an original resort at the Walt Disney World Resort that was never constructed?

8. How did Disney's Fort Wilderness Campground and Resort get its name?

9. What kind of airport was the former 2000-foot landing strip adjacent to the Walt Disney World Magic Kingdom main parking lot?

10. Where is Beachcomber Isle?

11. What island located at the Walt Disney World Resort was named Raz Island from 1900 to 1937?

12. What was the name of the little railroad that used to operate at Disney's Fort Wilderness Campground and Resort?

13. President Richard Nixon made what famous statement during a November 11, 1973, press conference held at Disney's Contemporary Resort?

14. Crockett's Tavern, located at Disney's Fort Wilderness Campground and Resort, played host to a character dining experience featuring which Country Bear Jamboree entertainer?

15. Which Magic Kingdom themed land is located closest to Disney's Contemporary Resort?

16. What popular actor helped Mickey and Minnie celebrate the grand opening of Disney's Grand Floridian Resort & Spa in June 1988?

17. What is the name of the musical group that performs at Disney's Grand Floridian Resort & Spa, playing selections of popular American music spotlighting the highly spirited beat of the teens, twenties, and early thirties?

18. Which restaurant located at Disney's Grand Floridian Resort & Spa is named after a Native American word that means "baby bear"?

19. The first moderately priced Walt Disney World resort was Disney's Caribbean Beach Resort, which opened in 1988. Each building carries the name of an island located in the Caribbean. How many different island names are featured at the resort?

20. What is the name of the body of water located at Disney's Caribbean Beach Resort?

21. Who is the fictitious adventurer and entrepreneur who supposedly helped inspire the development of Pleasure Island?

22. Which Disney water park was referred to as Splash during its planning stages?

23. Which were the first two Disney resorts to share a similar theme?

24. What is the name of the shipwrecked boat located at Disney's Yacht and Beach Club Resorts?

25. The Casting Center building, which is the home of all employment hiring at the Walt Disney World Resort, is inspired by which famous structure located in Venice, Italy?

26. What is the name of the building located at the Walt Disney World Resort that opened in 1991 and is designed to house the administrative staff all in one facility?

27. The musical notes that decorate the registration desk at Disney's Port Orleans Resort are notes found in what song?

28. Which Disney resort's main building has been designed to resemble an old-fashioned train station?

29. Where could one find Ol' Man Island?

30. Which Disneyland Paris resort is based on the concept of a gold-rush town in the Old West?

31. What three types of buildings are represented at the Disneyland Paris resort, Hotel New York?

32. What is the name of the walkway around the Seven Seas Lagoon which features ten-inch hexagonal bricks with inscriptions and dedications by Walt Disney World Resort guests?

33. Which Disney Resort was originally going to be dubbed the Cypress Point Lodge?

34. The musical notes featured in the main lobby of Disney's All-Star Music Resort are from what song?

35. The Volkswagen, Herbie, used in the film *Herbie Goes Bananas* (1980) is on display in which Downtown Disney restaurant?

36. In 1996, the Disney Village Resort officially changed its name to what?

37. What is considered the first moderately-priced convention hotel at the Walt Disney World Resort?

38. What is the name of the fifteen-acre lake adjacent to Disney's Coronado Springs Resort?

39. What is the name of the Downtown Disney West Side dining and concert facility created by Isaac Tigrett II?

40. In which themed restaurant located at Downtown Disney West Side does the Walt Disney Company maintain a 12 percent ownership interest?

41. Which famous chef known for his California-style cuisine operates a restaurant at Downtown Disney West Side?

42. Goofy's Grill located at the Downtown Disney Marketplace was replaced in 1997 by what soda fountain and shop?

43. What Denmark-based toy manufacturer opened its own merchandise location at Downtown Disney Marketplace in 1997?

44. In 1997, the Fireworks Factory located at Downtown Disney Pleasure Island was replaced by what country western dance and club venue?

45. In 1997, Flagler's Restaurant located at Disney's Grand Floridian Resort & Spa was replaced by what new dining experience?

46. What is the name of the original production performed at the Cirque du Soleil theater at Downtown Disney West Side?

47. Name the five themed buildings that comprise Disney's All-Star Movies Resort.

48. If you count all of the Dalmatians that appear on the two themed 101 Dalmatians buildings at Disney's All-Star Movies Resort including the large Pongo and Perdita, how many are there?

49. What is the name of the thirty-six-hole elf-sized miniature golf course located at the entrance to Disney's Blizzard Beach?

50. What is the first ticketed park the Walt Disney Company has ever closed?

51. The pool area at the Disneyland Hotel was redesigned in 1999 with inspiration from which full-length animated feature?

52. What is the name of the 750-room resort that marks the entrance to Disney's California Adventure?

53. What is the name of the entertainment district situated adjacent to Disneyland and Disney's California Adventure?

54. What is the name of the luxurious resort featured at the entrance to Tokyo DisneySea?

55. What is the name of the Walt Disney World resort scheduled to open in 2001 adjacent to Disney's Animal Kingdom?

Disney Resorts/ Other Attractions

Answers:

1. The first monorail trains were actually built at the Disney Studios in Burbank, California.
2. Disney's Contemporary Resort Hotel was called the Tempo Bay Resort in early plans.
3. Disney's Contemporary Resort was initially owned by the U.S. Steel Corporation.
4. The Venetian, Mediterranean, Asian, and Persian Resorts were some of the resort designs suggested for the Walt Disney World Resort.
5. Disney artist and Imagineer Mary Blair was responsible for the mural's design. The ninety-foot-tall mural depicts a Grand Canyon scene. The design was inspired by Native American motifs from prehistoric stone petroglyphs to Pueblo art to Navajo ceremonial sand paintings. Each ceramic tile is one-foot-square and was painted in California and then shipped to Florida. The entire project took over one and a half years to complete.
6. Disney's Polynesian Resort uses this saying as its motto. Aita Peatea means "There will be another day tomorrow just like today."
7. The Taj Mahal was the inspiration for a resort originally planned for the Walt Disney World Resort. The original structure was planned as a black palace, not white, like the real Taj Mahal.
8. Disney's Fort Wilderness Campground and Resort was named after the fort located on Tom Sawyer Island in Disneyland.
9. The 2000-foot landing strip was a STOLport, which stands for Short Takeoff and Landing port. The landing strip was part of the Walt Disney World property's original plan, designed to accommodate small aircraft carrying guests coming to the resort for the day. However, it was quickly realized that the property would see too much traffic and safety concerns would arise, so the landing strip had to be closed.

10. Beachcomber Isle is the closest island to Disney's Polynesian Resort in Seven Seas Lagoon. It was formerly home to a wave machine. One of the original plans for the Walt Disney World Resort was to host championship surfing events and, of course, with the Polynesian hotel in the background, what better backdrop? The wave machine never worked properly, so eventually the plan was scrapped. In 1987, Beachcomber Isle was converted into a reef for fish.

11. The island in Disney's Bay Lake, near River Country, and the previous home of a Disney nature preserve, was named Raz Island from 1900 to 1937, after a family who lived there. The island was also the home of Florida's first on-air personality, Radio Nick, in the late 1930s, who renamed it Idle Bay Isle. Disney purchased the island, which was a hunting retreat at the time, in 1965. In 1974, the island opened to guests as Treasure Island and in 1977 the name was changed to Discovery Island.

12. In 1973, the Fort Wilderness Railroad opened and continued in operation until 1977. Four brightly painted narrow-gauge locomotives transported guests around the campground and resort. After the railroad closed, two of the coaches were used at Pleasure Island as ticket booths.

13. President Richard M. Nixon made the famous statement, "I am not a crook," in a speech at Disney's Contemporary Resort.

14. Melvin the Moose Breakfast Show debuted in 1986. It has the distinction of being the first character breakfast at the Walt Disney World Resort.

15. Disney's Contemporary Resort is closest to Tomorrowland at the Magic Kingdom. During the development stages of Walt Disney World, the resort was considered an extension of the Tomorrowland theme. Disney's Polynesian was designed with the same thinking. Prior to the opening of Disney's Grand Floridian Resort & Spa, Disney's Polynesian was the closest to Adventureland and was considered an extension of its theme.

16. Burt Reynolds.

17. The Grand Floridian Society Orchestra.

18. Narcoossee's name comes from a Native American word in the Osceola and Creek language that means "baby bear." Narcoossee is also the name of a town located just outside the Walt Disney World Resort. The restaurant was originally going to be called Narcoossee Nick's. Nick would have been the restaurant's fictitious personality who was ready to entertain and tell his tales of adventure.

19. Five: Aruba, Barbados, Jamaica, Martinique, and Trinidad. However, the name Trinidad is used twice to describe the buildings of Trinidad North and Trinidad South.

20. Barefoot Bay.

21. As the story goes, Merriweather Adam Pleasure was an adventurer and entrepreneur who enjoyed traveling the world. Pleasure had a successful sail-making business, but in 1941 he was lost at sea as he attempted to sail around the globe. He was never to be seen again. As the years passed, the island fell into ruin after a hurricane severely damaged the existing buildings. Imagineers eventually cleared the debris and overgrown jungle and rebuilt the island maintaining the original Pleasure philosophy for good entertainment and turned the idle buildings into nightclubs.

22. During its early development stages, Typhoon Lagoon was referred to as Splash.

23. Disney's Yacht and Beach Club Resorts.

24. The name of the shipwrecked boat is the *Albatross*. The boat serves as the slide for the resort's main pool area, Stormalong Bay.

25. The Rialto Bridge in Venice, Italy, helped provide the inspiration for the Casting Center building at the Walt Disney World Resort.

26. The facility is known as the Team Disney Building. Japanese architect Arata Isozaki designed the structure. Isozaki's design work on the Team Disney Building won the National Honor Award from the American Institute of Architects. Isozaki may best be known for his design of the Museum of Contemporary Art in Los Angeles, California.

27. The song featured in musical notes at Disney's Port Orleans Resort is "When the Saints Go Marching In."

28. The main building of Disney's Old Key West Resort has been designed to resemble an old-fashioned train station.

29. Ol' Man Island is located at Disney's Dixie Landings Resort. The story behind the location revolves around a tale of an old man who settled in the area in 1835 and built it up as a bustling waterfront community.

30. The Cheyenne Hotel was inspired by the concept of a gold-rush town in the Old West.

31. The three styles represented at Hotel New York are the skyscrapers of Manhattan, the brownstones found on Park Avenue, and the row houses of Gramercy Park.

32. Disney's Walk Around the World.

33. Disney's Wilderness Lodge was originally going to be called Cypress Point Lodge.

34. The musical notes that appear in the main lobby of Disney's All-Star Music Resort are from "When You Wish Upon a Star."

35. Herbie, The Love Bug can be seen hanging from the rafters of Planet Hollywood located at Downtown Disney Pleasure Island. Exhibits from other Disney films include Daryl Hannah's mermaid tail from the 1984 film *Splash* and the Santa Claus suit worn by Tim Allen in the 1994 motion picture *The Santa Clause.*

36. On February 9, 1996, the Disney Village Resort officially became known as the Disney Institute. Along with their traditional resort accommodations, guests have the opportunity to attend classes and seminars covering a variety of subjects including rock climbing, Disney animation, and culinary specialties.

37. In 1997, Disney's Coronado Springs Resort opened, becoming the first moderately priced convention hotel located at the Walt Disney World Resort.

38. The fifteen-acre lake adjacent to Disney's Coronado Springs Resort is known as Lago Dorado.

39. Isaac Tigrett II, originator of the Hard Rock Café, developed the concept for the House of Blues. The House of Blues features a restaurant specializing in Mississippi Delta cuisine and a 2,000 seat performance hall showcasing live concerts and the best in rhythm and blues, jazz, and gospel music.

40. The Walt Disney Company maintains a 12 percent ownership interest in the House of Blues restaurant.

41. Wolfgang Puck.

42. Goofy's Grill was replaced in 1997 by the Ghirardelli Soda Fountain and Chocolate Shop. Ghirardelli, the San Francisco-based confectionary, has been known as one of the country's premier candy makers for over one hundred years.

43. Lego Systems, Inc., the Denmark-based toy company, opened its second permanent exhibition in the United States at Downtown Disney Marketplace. The Lego Imagination Center opened in 1997.

44. The Wildhorse Saloon, known for its unique brand of country-western music featuring live performances by some of the industry's up-and-coming new acts, replaced the Fireworks Factory.

45. Cítricos replaced Flagler's at Disney's Grand Floridian Resort & Spa.

46. The high-energy original production, which includes more than sixty artists from around the world including gymnasts, acrobats, dancers, and clowns, is known as La Nouba. La Nouba is derived from the French expression *faire la Nouba* which means "to party, to live it up."

47. The five themed buildings are: Fantasia, 101 Dalmatians, The Love Bug, The Mighty Ducks, and Toy Story.

48. There are actually 101 Dalmatians that appear at the two buildings.

49. The miniature golf course is known as Disney's Winter Summerland. The elf-sized golf course is divided into two eighteen-hole courses. One course carries the zany, snow-clad Florida look reminiscent of Disney's Blizzard Beach, while the other has a more tropical holiday theme with ornaments hanging from palm trees.

50. On April 8, 1999, the eleven-acre zoological park Discovery Island closed. The park closed nearly a year after Disney's Animal Kingdom opened. The island was home to more than 130 species of animals, including Galapagos turtles and ring-tailed lemurs. The island opened in 1974.

51. The completely redesigned pool area located at the Disneyland Hotel is known as the Never Land Pool inspired by the 1953 feature *Peter Pan*.
52. Disney's Grand Californian Hotel.
53. The entertainment district, complete with restaurants and clubs, is known as Downtown Disney.
54. The resort is known as Tokyo DisneySea Hotel MiraCosta. The hotel itself represents the elegant and rustic architecture of four different regions of Italy.
55. The resort is known as Disney's Animal Kingdom Lodge.

Walt Disney and His Legacy

Questions:

1. In which of the following professions did Walt Disney's father, Elias, *not* work at some point in his life: carpenter, contractor, newspaper distributor, hotel manager, or farmer?

2. Walt Disney's father worked as a carpenter for which World's Fair?

3. What kind of farm animal, which he called Skinny, did Walt Disney have as a child?

4. What 1916 silent film provided Walt Disney with the inspiration to produce his first full-length animated feature?

5. True or false: the house, designed by their mother and built by their father, in which Walt Disney and Roy Disney were born still stands.

6. What occupations did Walt Disney's older brothers Herbert and Raymond hold?

7. Who operated the first animation studio in Hollywood?

8. What famous actress once wrote a note to Walt Disney asking the question, "Mr. Disney, why do you wait so long between Mickey Mouse appearances?"

9. What famous director used Disney-animated maps in a famous series of propaganda films during World War II?

10. True or false: at one point during World War II, 93 percent of the Disney Studios resources were engaged in special government work, including the production of training and propaganda films for the armed services as well as health films.

11. Who said, "Donald is a very outrageous fellow, with bad manners and a worse temper. And everyone is very fond of him, including myself"?

12. Which company has produced Disney character plush toys longer than anyone?

13. Roy O. Disney presented an animation cel from which 1952 cartoon to Emperor Hirohito of Japan?

14. The head of what pioneering chain of hamburger restaurants asked Walt Disney in 1954 about the possibility of opening one of his fast food locations in Disneyland park?

15. What slang term did Walt Disney use for the large focal landmarks in each land in his theme park which one can see from the central hub?

16. Who said, "I love Mickey as much as any woman"?

17. On March 30, 1957, Walt Disney helped dedicate a school that was named after him in the Magnolia School District of Anaheim, California. What announcement, to the dismay of school administrators, did Walt make to the students during his dedication speech?

18. In what decade did Disney stock reach a financial milestone when it moved from being a mere over-the-counter (OTC) stock to being listed on the New York Stock Exchange?

19. Walt Disney provided the narration for what attraction at the 1964–1965 New York World's Fair?

20. The Tower of the Four Winds was a 120-foot kinetic structure erected to mark the entrance to what attraction at the 1964–1965 New York World's Fair?

21. What two people have affectionately been referred to as Walt Disney's "Supercalifragilistic Songwriting Team"?

22. The Disney Company received its first Grammy Awards for the music in what motion picture?

23. After Walt Disney sold WED Enterprises, his personal company, to Walt Disney Productions, what did he use as the name for his new company, formed to handle the family's interests? (Hint: It comes from his name.)

24. In what year was the press conference held when Walt Disney officially announced his plans to build a vast entertainment enterprise in Florida?

25. Which Disney song did the Disneyland band play during the flag-lowering ceremony in tribute to Walt Disney on the occasion of his untimely death on December 15, 1966?

26. In how many different states did Walt Disney live during his lifetime?

27. Who made the decision to name the new Florida project Walt Disney World as opposed to just Disney World?

28. In what decade was CEO and chairman Michael D. Eisner born?

29. At what TV network in New York did Michael Eisner get his first job in the entertainment industry?

30. At what sporting event was the popular ad campaign introduced featuring star athletes exclaiming "I'm going to Disneyland" or "I'm going to Disney World"?

31. What was the first year Disney led all Hollywood studios in box office receipts?

32. What distinguished award did chairman and CEO Michael Eisner receive from the government of France years after Walt Disney received the same honor?

33. What Academy Award–winning actor was appointed to The Walt Disney Company board of directors after the untimely death of Frank G. Wells in 1994?

34. In December 1994, The Walt Disney Company had the top-grossing film in theaters, *The Santa Clause,* the highest-rated television program, *Home Improvement,* and the number one nonfiction book on the *New York Times* best-seller list, *Don't Stand Too Close to a Naked Man.* What do these three have in common?

35. Which state's capital dedicated a bust of Walt Disney as an honorary citizen of the state?

36. Which of the following cable networks is not partially or fully owned by The Walt Disney Company: A & E, The History Channel, or ESPN?

37. In what year was the town of Celebration officially dedicated?

38. Who has been credited with coming up with the name Celebration for Disney's planned community on the southernmost portion of the Walt Disney World Resort?

39. What is the title of the recording released in 1996 featuring contemporary country artists singing Disney classics?

40. What is the name of the twenty-four-hour children's radio network launched by the Disney company in 1996?

41. What is the title of the mountain-climbing book written by former president of The Walt Disney Company, Frank G. Wells?

42. October 16, 1998, marked what impressive milestone for The Walt Disney Company?

43. In what century was Lillian Disney born?

44. What is the name of the cable network launched by the Disney Company in 1998 that specializes in cartoons?

45. What Disney family member was recognized in 1998 with his own star on Hollywood's legendary Walk of Fame?

46. What is the title of the book written by author Bob Thomas that details the life of Disney company cofounder Roy O. Disney?

47. What veteran Disney artist is responsible for painting Mickey Mouse's official portraits?

48. What is the title of chairman and CEO Michael Eisner's autobiography, released in 1998?

49. What is the name of The Walt Disney Company's new Web site that debuted on the Internet on January 12, 1999?

50. In October, 1999, the Disney company announced plans to build a new theme park in what country?

Walt Disney and His Legacy

Answers:

1. Walt Disney's father, Elias, tried his hand at all of these professions at some point in his life. He worked as a carpenter and contractor in Chicago, had a newspaper franchise in Kansas City, managed the Halifax Hotel in Daytona Beach, and was a farmer in Marceline, Missouri.

2. Elias Disney worked as a carpenter for $1 a day at the 1893 World's Columbian Exposition in Chicago.

3. Walt Disney used to have a pig, which he called Skinny, on his Marceline farm.

4. In 1916, Walt Disney viewed a silent film version of *Snow White* in Kansas City starring actress Marguerite Clark. The motion picture later provided Walt with the inspiration for the development of his first full-length animated feature *Snow White and the Seven Dwarfs* (1937).

5. True. The house is on Tripp Avenue in Chicago.

6. Walt Disney's brother Herbert spent his career working for the United States Postal Service and his brother Raymond held several different jobs, but he was primarily an insurance agent.

7. Roy and Walt Disney. The Disney Brothers Cartoon Studio became the first Hollywood-based animation studio in 1923. At that time, most animation studios were based in New York City.

8. Legendary actress and screen star Mary Pickford.

9. Frank Capra, in such films as *Battle of Britain* and *War Comes to America*. Capra may best be remembered for directing such classic films as *Mr. Smith Goes to Washington* (1939) and *It's a Wonderful Life* (1946).

10. True. Walt Disney recognized that it was his duty to do as much as he could to support the war effort, so he offered the resources of his studios. In one particular case, Disney artists designed over 1,200 military insignias for the different branches and units of the armed services. Remarkably, some of the health films produced by the Disney Studios are still being shown in parts of the world by the U.S. State Department.

11. Walt Disney.

12. The Gund Manufacturing Co., as it was called then, began manufacturing Disney character plush toys in 1947. Over the years, other companies such as the Ideal Toy Company, Character Novelty, and Knickerbocker have also produced plush toys for Disney. The Gund Company was the exclusive supplier of Winnie the Pooh wearing the traditional small red shirt for Sears Roebuck & Company.

13. Roy O. Disney presented an animation cel to Emperor Hirohito from the 1952 animated short *Lambert, The Sheepish Lion*.

14. The letter was from Ray A. Kroc, head of McDonald's Corporation. Interestingly, forty-three years later a McDonald's restaurant did open on the grounds of the Walt Disney World Resort.

15. Walt Disney referred to the Fantasyland castle, the Tomorrowland rocket ship, and the riverboat in Frontierland as "wienies." Walt planned these attractions to catch the eye and draw visitors into the land from the central hub. The reference to wienies came from the Mack Sennett movies, where a neighborhood dog would pull a wagon while encouraged by a hot dog on the end of a stick.

16. Walt Disney.

17. Walt Disney invited all of the children to take a day off from school and come to Disneyland as his guests.

18. The 1950s. It was on November 12, 1957.

19. Walt Disney provided the narration for Ford's Magic Skyway. Guests traveled through the attraction in a Ford car and Walt's voice was heard over the car's radio.

20. The Tower of the Four Winds marked the entrance to It's a Small World.

21. Richard and Robert Sherman, because they wrote the song "Supercalifragilisticexpialidocious."

22. *Mary Poppins* (1964) received two Grammy Awards—one for "Best Original Score" and one for "Best Recording for Children."

23. Retlaw Enterprises. Spelled backwards the name is "Walter."

24. On November 15, 1965, Walt Disney, his brother Roy, and then Governor Haydon Burns announced the Florida project. Included in the announcement were plans for a Disneyland-type theme park, recreation areas, and two cities, one traditional and one futuristic.

25. The band played "When You Wish Upon a Star."

26. Three: Illinois, Missouri, and California. Walt Disney was born in Chicago, Illinois. At age four, his family moved to Marceline, Missouri. When Walt turned nine, his family then moved to Kansas City, Missouri. At age fifteen, Walt's family again moved back to Chicago, and a year later after serving some time in France with the American Red Cross Ambulance Corps, he was back in Kansas City, Missouri. Finally, at the age of twenty-one, Walt Disney made his final move to California, where he lived for the remainder of his life.

27. It was Walt's brother Roy who insisted that the new property be known as Walt Disney World. Roy wanted the world to know that its creation represented the dreams of his brother.

28. The 1940s; Michael Eisner was born on March 7, 1942.

29. During summer recess while attending Denison University, Michael Eisner got his first job in the entertainment industry working as a page for NBC, answering phones, giving studio tours, running errands, and showing audience members to their seats on game shows such as *The Price Is Right*.

30. The Super Bowl. The ad campaign was introduced in 1987 after the New York Giants victory in Super Bowl XXI over the Denver Broncos. The athlete featured in that first commercial was Giants' quarterback Phil Simms. The ad campaign was suggested by Michael Eisner's wife, Jane.

31. It wasn't until 1987 that Disney led all other Hollywood studios in box office receipts, primarily as a result of such motion pictures as *Three Men and a Baby* and *Good Morning, Vietnam*.

32. Michael Eisner received the distinguished Legion d'Honneur award from the government of France.

33. Actor Sidney Poitier took the Board seat vacated by the sudden death of Frank G. Wells.

34. Tim Allen starred in the film and television program and authored the book.

35. Missouri's state capital, Jefferson City, dedicated a bust of Walt Disney to recognize his contribution to the state.

36. Actually, The Walt Disney Company has an interest in all of the cable networks listed.

37. The town of Celebration was officially dedicated by Michael Eisner on July 4, 1996.

38. Michael Eisner's wife, Jane Eisner.

39. The recording is known as "The Best of Country Sings the Best of Disney." The CD also captured the company's first Grammy nomination in the country music category. Alison Krauss's rendition of "Baby Mine" from the animated feature *Dumbo* (1941) earned a Best Female and Country Vocal Performance nomination.

40. In November 1996, Radio Disney was launched in four test markets. Radio Disney is a live twenty-four-hour children's radio network complete with music, kid-friendly news, sports, and feature programming for children under twelve.

41. Frank G. Wells wrote *Seven Summits*, detailing his quest to climb the highest mountains on each of the seven continents.

42. The date marked the seventy-fifth anniversary of The Walt Disney Company.

43. Lillian Disney was born in the nineteenth century (in 1899). She lived to age ninety-eight.

44. Toon Disney was launched as a new cable network, an offshoot of The Disney Channel, on April 18, 1998.

45. Disney company cofounder Roy O. Disney received his star posthumously in 1998 on Hollywood's legendary Walk of Fame. Walt Disney was already recognized on the Walk of Fame with two stars of his own.

46. The title of the book is *Building a Company: Roy O. Disney and the Creation of an Entertainment Empire*. Bob Thomas is also the author of *Walt Disney: An American Original* and *The Art of Animation*. Thomas is also the first author-journalist to be recognized with his own star on Hollywood's legendary Walk of Fame.

47. John Hench is responsible for creating Mickey's official portraits celebrating his twenty-fifth, fiftieth, and sixtieth anniversaries, and, most recently, his seventieth. Hench is a senior vice president for Walt Disney Imagineering and has been with The Walt Disney Company for over sixty years.

48. The title of the book is *Work in Progress*, written with Tony Schwartz.

49. The Web site is known as GO Network and it is designed to increase the company's presence on the Internet by combining forces with Infoseek's existing portal (a site that serves as a point of origin).

50. In October, 1999 the Disney company announced plans to build a second theme park in France adjacent to Disneyland Paris. In November of the same year, the company announced plans to build a theme park in Hong Kong.